THE FARM SHOW

THE FARM SHOW

A COLLECTIVE CREATION BY
THEATRE PASSE MURAILLE

COACH HOUSE

THE FARM SHOW

This is a record of our version of 'grass roots' theatre. The idea was to take a group of actors out to a farming community and build a play of what we could see and learn. There is no 'story' or 'plot' as such. The form of the play is more like a Canadian Sunday School or Christmas Concert where one person does a recitation, another sings a song, a third acts out a skit, etc. Nevertheless, we hope that you can see many stories woven into the themes of this play and that out of it will emerge a picture of a complex and living community.

The play was not written down; it developed out of interviews, visits, and improvisations. Most of the words used were given to us by the community along with their stories. We spent a great deal of our time trying to imitate these people both in the way they move and the way they speak. We wanted to capture the fibre of what they were and this seemed the best way to do it. In any case, it taught us to watch and listen. I'm not sure how much of this will come through the printed word.

PAUL THOMPSON

Usually a script is the first hint of a play's existence. In this case, it is the last.

In the early days of that summer of '72, the actors had no idea what they were doing. The dramatic techniques, and the songs grew out of the actors' attempts to dramatize their discoveries in daily improvisational sessions. At first the result didn't seem like a play: no lights, no costumes, no set, a barn for a theatre, haybales for seats. Simply pure performance. First in those incredible performances at Clinton, and then again in Toronto, in Saskatchewan, in Southern Ontario auction barns, in the palatial art centres of Ottawa, Stratford, and Manitoba, Michael Ondaatje's successful film, a CBC television special, several radio versions, and finally crowds of strangers asking, 'How did you do this?' No one anticipated the delight people would take in hearing their own language and observing their own culture. As John Coulter (author of the play 'Riel') said, 'It's like Ireland in the twenties. The people are discovering themselves.'

Ted Johns

(L-R) Paul Thompson, David Fox, Anne Anglin, Severn, Fina MacDonnell,
Miles Potter, Al Jones, Christopher, Janet Amos

Original cast: Janet Amos, Ann Anglin, David Fox, Al Jones, Fina MacDonell, Miles Potter. Directed by Paul Thompson, Theatre Passe Muraille. Stage design by Ed Fisher. The music was composed by Anne Anglin and is available from Theatre Passe Muraille on request.

Photographs were taken by Al Jones, Gary McKeehan, and Robert Nasmith.

Other references:

'Interview with Paul Thompson', *Performing Arts*, Vol. x, No. 4, pp. 30-32.

'The Farm Show': a one hour tape available from Robert Weaver, CBC Radio, Toronto.

'The Clinton Special': a documentary film by Michael Ondaatje available from the Toronto Filmmakers Co-operative, 341 Bloor St. W., Toronto.

This script was prepared by Ted Johns. All songs and poems in this play were composed by members of the original cast. Except for 'The Laughing Song'. That, as far as I know, is Clark Johnson's.

ACT I

ACT II

We would like to dedicate this play to the farmers near Clinton, and especially to:

Sally Bird
Ray Bird
Les Jervis
Alison Lobb
Alma Lobb
Bill Lobb
Bruce Lobb
Diane Lobb
Don Lobb
Jean Lobb
Mervin Lobb
Millie Lobb
Jack Merrill
Lula Merrill
William Rueger
Carmen Tebbutt
J. Chas. Wilson

All the characters in this play are non fictional. Any resemblance to living people is purely intentional.

Jack Merrill

Beulah Lodge, Fordwich Ontario

Act i, Scene i. Introduction.

> *One of the more easy-going members of the cast is present onstage for
> about an hour before the show begins helping people find seats, talking
> to them, or listening to the country fiddle music (which was
> frequently supplied by local musicians, especially when the show was
> on tour through rural areas). During the last ten minutes or so the
> other members of the cast gradually move onstage and take up their
> positions sitting on the bales waiting for the introduction (which took
> various forms but, when playing to city audiences, went something
> like this):*

Last summer we visited a farming community near Clinton, Ontario.
Clinton is about a hundred and twenty miles due west of Toronto.
You go down to Kitchener and then take the number eight highway to
Stratford, Mitchell, Seaforth, *Clinton*. Which would be right about
here (just off the front of stage left) if it were on this map.

It's a nice town of about three thousand people, but people blast on
through it along the number eight, past the village of Holmesville and
on up to *Goderich* (just off the front of stage right). Because Goderich is
on Lake Huron, it's the county seat, and that's where the tourists want
to get to. Now beside the number eight highway is the community we
lived in. This map (*marked on naked stage*) shows the roads and the
names of the different farmers in the area.

We lived there for about six weeks and put this show on for the
people there. They seemed to enjoy it so we brought it back to see if
we could brighten up the dull lives of the people who live in Toronto.

We also brought back a few things from Clinton.

This is part of a bean dryer.

These are straw bales, not to be confused with the hay bales you'll
hear about later.

An old cream can. Some crates. An actual Clinton shopping cart.

The show kind of bounces along one way or another and then it
stops. You've got a ten-minute intermission coming up so you can rest
your frazzled nerves, and get clear of those seats which I gather aren't
all that comfortable. But then you come back. And you seat through
the second half. That's about all you need to know except to say that
this show was first performed in a barn which belongs to Ray Bird. So
we'd like to welcome this audience to the Ray Bird Memorial Theatre
Production of *The Farm Show*!

> *Auction song cuts in immediately.*

Stomp, clap! Stomp, clap! Stomp, clap! clap!
Stomp, clap! Stomp, clap! Stomp, clap! clap!

*This rhythm is maintained by the cast at a fast pace during the chorus
and at a slower pace during the verses of the 'Auction song'.*

CHORUS
Auction song:
Pound for 25, 25, 30
Pound for 25, 30, 35
Pound for 35, 35, 40
Pound for 45, 50, 55!

Verse one (Part 1 – Sung)
Down in Huron County every Friday night
Man from thirty miles around is holding on real tight
To his backside pocket where he keeps ten hundred bills
There'll be some fancy countin' on the county auction tills
Yes on the county auction tills.

(Part 2 – Spoken)
They'll be bidding sows and fillies – their faces still as stone,
Every move's another dollar, they won't smile till they get home,
No, they won't smile till they get home …

CHORUS
Verse two (Part 1 – Sung)
There's a Giant in the ring he's drinking whiskey-Seven-Up
He's got a stick to show the stock that he's a cop.
Got to keep them moving – there can be no standing still.
Biped over four legs – there's a way when there's a will
Yes there's a way when there's a will.

(Part 2 – Spoken)
Now somehow a leg got broken, he holds the sow up by her tail,
He pats her rump to soothe her; he won't have to make the kill;
No he won't have to make the kill.

CHORUS
Verse three (Part 1 – Sung)
Then there's cardboard Mary and she's whispering to Sue,
They're sitting in the gallery they've got the best view

A curly stud is standing at the nearest entrance gate,
He's fixed his eyes upon them he's imagining his fate
Imagining his fate.

(Part 2 – Spoken)
Her mother's sitting over on the far side of the ring
She knows her girl is growing, but she doesn't see a thing
No she doesn't see a thing.

CHORUS
Verse four (Part 1 – Sung)
Johnny Johnson's sitting with his wife and boy and babe
Missus is bouncing happy with the family they've made.
Grandma holds the bottle, Grandpa bids on four boars
Gives his name, winks at his son then, turns around for more
Then he turns around for more,

(Part 2 – Sung)
Here comes Cash Crop Jennings, he's as big as seven bales,
He'll tell a funny story if the lady turns away.
Baptist Tom says 'stick around, I'm pushin' up the pound'
Jennings drops his grin and says you don't need me around
Well now, you don't need me around …

CHORUS
Verse five (Part 1 – Sung)
Pigs and goats and ponies, Hereford steers and boars
Elephants, performing bears, dogs and lion roar;
Robin saw the circus when it came to Goderich town,
He's going to be an acrobat or possibly a clown
Or possibly a clown,

(Part 2 – Spoken)
And while his dad is nodding at the silver microphone,
The kid may get a pony that will be his very own,
That will be his very own.

CHORUS
(concludes with) Sold!

> *The actors change into the farm animals at the auction and the
> stockman of verse two chases them off-stage with appropriate noises,
> leaving behind the actor who will play Mr Merrill in Scene Two
> following.*

Act I, Scene II. Miles meets Mr Merrill.

Jack Merrill is working onstage moving his bales at an even pace throughout the scene. Miles works eagerly but in fits and starts.

MILES
(offstage) Mr. Merrill? *(pause)* Mr. Merrill?

JACK
Yep.

MILES
(enters) Oh, there you are. Hi, my name's Miles Potter. *(pause)*.

JACK
Uh huh! *(pause.)*
MILES
I'm ... from Toronto.

JACK
Uh, huh.

MILES
We're up here, you see, because we're going to do this play about farming ...

JACK
Oh!?

MILES
... and we thought that as part of it we would go around to different farmers and see if we could be of some use.

JACK
Ah hah!

MILES
(pause) ...ah *(embarrassed laugh)* ah ... could I be of some use?

JACK
Sure, those bales need stacking over here.

MILES
Oh sure, yeh! *(Very eager. He carries the bale awkwardly in both arms.)*

JACK
Generally, we carry those by the twine ...

MILES
The what?

JACK
The string.

MILES
Oh. That sure is a lot easier. *(pause)* I guess you know a lot of tricks like that!
(pause) Boy, it sure must be great being a farmer ...

JACK
Oh!?

MILES
I mean you get up in the morning and get your hands down into that good honest dirt. What time do you get up in the morning Mr Merrill?

JACK
Oh, six, sometimes earlier.

MILES
Six! Eh. *(a little surprised, pause)* Boy, this sure is a great old barn, Mr Merrill. *(whistles)* Hand-hewn beams! I'll bet it's one of those antique barns.

JACK
It's pretty old I guess.

MILES
Sure would like to get some of these boards ... take them back to Toronto and make a coffee table out of them. *(pause)*

JACK
We'll go in and get some supper now.

MILES

Look, if there's anything you want to do … dig some posts, plant some corn, anything.

JACK

No, we'll have our supper first.

MILES

Oh, you mean like organic vegetables from your garden and all, far out!

JACK

Well, we eat where we scratch. *(exit)*

MILES

(to audience) What?

> *Blackout if there are lights being used in the production. If not, freeze for 'a thousand and one, a thousand and two'. Then all actors enter in character for scene three following.*

Act I, Scene III. Round the Bend.

The title refers to the bend in the road. This scene is a series of images of the people in the area at their work. All actors are visible at all times, carrying out the activities of one or another of their characters.

JANET

These *(Other actors freeze)* are the two concession lines where we got to know most of the farmers this summer. This *(pointing to the map drawn on the stage)* is the sixteenth line going down to highway eight, and this is the Maitland line which runs down to those cross-roads right down there. The farm house we stayed in is right here. It was about a hundred and twenty years old, and it was given to us for the summer by a farmer named Ray Bird. Now, *he* lived down here on highway eight and he farmed the land ...

RAY BIRD

Well. *(Janet freezes. Other actors stay in freeze.)* You know. The way it used to be, I'd be sitting around in the winter time ... and my *conscience*, and my wife, would prod me to get to work. So I would. But now, it's just the opposite. I'll be riding along on my tractor, and my conscience ... will prod me ... to stop. So I'll get off. Sit under a tree. Look at the sky. Think. *(Movement and sound)*

CARMEN TEBBUTT

Oh ... *(Other actors freeze)* I don't know that you'd call us progressive farmers. Of course we've had our share of hard knocks, heh, heh. We're Mr and Mrs Carmen Tebbutt and we live on the corner of Highway eight and the sixteenth. We sold the farm to the young Lobb lad up the line. Of course, we still live in the house ... She used to help me out on the tractor ... till there got to be too many ground-hog holes, heh, heh. We used to get up at four o'clock in the morning and take the wagon around to all the other farms and pick up the cans of milk and take them down to the dairy at Holmesville. *(Movement and sound. Actors change into chickens which Lula feeds during her speech.)*

LULA MERRILL

Now, Lois is our youngest but she got married first. Well that's the way things happen sometimes. One cute thing with Lois' wedding ... they took a ride in the wheel-barrow after the ceremony ... around the town so's everybody could get a look. Now, with Fay's wedding, they cleaned up the manure spreader with 'International' on the side, and they painted it red and white. Well, that's the colours that Fay wanted. We had to be careful with that 'cause red's a hard colour to match. *(Movement and sound continues until Stephen's ball is returned.)*

STEPHEN LOBB

Can you catch! *(runs to the front of the stage)* Can you *catch? (throws ball into the audience and carries on in character until they throw it back)* Thanks. *(Other actors freeze.)* My name is Stephen Lobb and I was just out in the field picking milkweed so my dad can combine it. Well, we were only told to do it for an hour, so that's all we did. I want to be a hockey player when I grow up! ... Oh ... I don't think I'd be a farmer. Well, I guess I would if it was the last thing I could do.

ALMA LOBB

Now, you get out of those roses. *(Stephen dashes to stage right, freezes. Other actors stay in freeze.)* Well, it's not the best time of the year for roses, but we don't want them squashed. I'm Alma Lobb, and I live here next door to my son, Bill. My husband is dead now. I built this rock garden myself. This hill was just a mess when I came, and I put in the rocks and the little pond there. I don't like the frogs to come round, but they do. It's not very good this year. There's been a lot of rain and I'm not as young as I was ... well, you can see that yucca tree there. *(Points to one of the actors in appropriate freeze.)* It only has one bloom this year. It usually has three or four. Well, you'll have to excuse me. I have to go in and wash my dishes. My grandchildren are coming over and I have to ... *(Movement and sound)*

BETTY FEAGAN

Oh, hi! *(Other actors freeze)* Come on in! No, we're not busy. We saw the light on over there. We knew you were there but we didn't go over. You know, we didn't know what to expect. You must be Janet. Look who's here, Ross!

ROSS FEAGAN

Hi! I'm Ross Feagan. I guess you met my wife, Betty.

BETTY FEAGAN

Excuse my hair. I've been out in the barn.

ROSS FEAGAN

That's all right Betty. Hey! I bet you can't guess what this is. *(pointing*

Fina as Diane Lobb

to bean dryer) No! You're wrong. That's the first span of a bridge I'm building over my new fish pond. It's a hundred and twenty five feet long, sixteen feet deep. I'm gonna fill her up with speckled trout!

BETTY FEAGAN

We're gonna make a lot of money, aren't we, Ross.

ROSS FEAGAN

Sure are, Betty. Those Yankee tourists'll pay sixty cents an inch just to pull them out.

BETTY FEAGAN

Say, would you like a coffee and a tomato sandwich?

ROSS FEAGAN

Oh, sure! Come on in. If there's one thing Betty can do besides take care of the pigs, it's bake bread. Now, come on in! *(Move upstage.)*

WILLIAM RUEGER

My name *(Feagan freezes)* is William Rueger. I live on the sixteenth line across from the abandoned schoolhouse. *(William takes hold of the extended arms of actor bent over to create his garden tractor which moves slowly forward with appropriate noises during the following lines.)*

My boys have all left home now. My youngest is out west I think. I haven't heard from him in a long time.

My wife died last year so my eleven year old daughter is looking after the house now.

I have fifty acres I'd like to sell for twenty thousand dollars if I could get an offer like that.

But, you know. With the price my piglets are getting this year I don't really care whether I sell the farm or not! *(Movement and sound)*

ROBBA LOBB

Hi. *(Other actors freeze. Robba; shy, feminine, playing croquet.)* We just got this croquet set this summer. Murray and I teach school. But this summer I don't have to take any more courses. So I guess we'll just … play croquet. We were both brought up on farms. But you need a lot of money … and good land, so I guess we'll just add on to the house. You know, every time he takes his turn, he knocks my ball way out into the field. Well, you do. But, watch this. *(takes careful aim and swings, hitting the imaginary ball with appropriate sound which is cue for other actors to start into movement and sound)*

HARRY OAKES

Hunh! Crop insurance! *(Other actors freeze)* That would take all the challenge out of farming!

HERB OAKES

Hi. *(smiles)* My name is Herb Oakes. And this is my father, Harry.

HARRY OAKES

How d'you do? We live at the bend of the sixteenth and the Maitland. We're building a new sow barn. My boy Herb took a welding course down in London last year and we're doing most of the work ourselves. Should have room for forty or fifty geld, eh Herb? *(Herb continues to smile with his arms folded. Says nothing.)*

HARRY OAKES

Improvements!? Oh, I don't know about more improvements. I don't think so ... What do you think, Herb? *(Herb Oakes continues to smile, unfolds his arms, shrugs, and starts to turn away. Movement and sound.)*

WENDY BIRD

Wendy Bird. *(Other actors freeze)* Oh ... I hate the farm. There's nothing to *do* around here. Clinton's a real greaser town. I'm going to university in the fall and I want to be a social worker. I don't think I'll come back here when I graduate. I'd like to go out west, maybe to Winnipeg to work.

MRS TEBBUTT

Oh ... kids to-day! They don't know what they want to do – take my son, for instance. He's twenty-one years old and now he's decided he's going back to school to get his grade thirteen. Well his girlfriend talked him into that. He says she didn't, but I know she did. It's always the women. But don't tell him I said so, eh?

Oh, I used to work. I used to work for Shaeffer Pen with Betty Feagan down the road there – but, ohh, I got sick and had an operation, and then we went on strike, and I never went back. And I'm glad. Because now I can do things when I want to do them. *(Movement and sound)*

> *Crates, mailbox, or whatever, for* WINTER SCENE *following are moved into position during the movement/sound sequences between the following speeches.*

ROBIN THOMPSON

Facts! *(Other actors freeze)* So you want to know some *facts* about farming!? Well, I'll tell you some facts about farming. Name's Thompson. Robin Thompson. I'm the township council clerk and the second most successful farmer in this area. Now the fact is: a farmer lives poor and dies rich. Most of the time he doesn't have a dime in his pocket. Looks like a welfare bum. And then he dies – and he's worth fifty, seventy-five, a hundred, sometimes two hundred thousand dollars. And I can cite you examples of that one for one up and down the line. That's a fact: a farmer lives poor and dies rich. *(Movement and sound)*

DIANE LOBB

Jacka! *(Other actors freeze)* Jacka! Oh ... hello. I'm Diane Lobb. I live up there with my husband Bruce and our three children. Well, some of our relatives probably think that we're religious fanatics. But, well, we were saved about a year ago. I don't know if you know what I *mean* when I say that we were *saved*. It's just that we opened our hearts and accepted Jesus as our own personal saviour. And our life has changed so much since we've been saved. *(Movement and sound)*

HARRY THOMPSON

(Harsh growling and barking of dog. Other actors freeze) Ohhh, don't worry about him. He won't bite. He's gentle as a lamb. Harry Thompson's the name. Live catta-corner to Robin Thompson. Yah, I farm, but I like to collect old things as well. You take this crate for example. This crate belonged to one of the first settlers in Huron County. Here's an interesting item. *(carelessly picks up an old mailbox or whatever)* Nobody knows exactly what this is – not even the experts! I found it in an old Indian burial ground. Nobody knows where that burial ground is either – not even my wife. And I'm not telling her. Ohhh, if I weren't a farmer, I suppose I'd be an artifact collector. *(Movement and sound)*

SALLY BIRD

Oh. *(Other actors are now offstage except for actor who will play the husband in the* WINTER SCENE.*)* Was that for me? It was? Oh, well, that's all right. I was busy. Yes. Oh, hello. I'm Sally Bird. Naomi just answered a telephon call for me and I would have liked to have taken it, because ... well, you see, in the summer, for a week, I run a single parent day-camp and ... oh ... Rosemary, where are you going ... well, please, would you do the dishes? ... I know. Thank-you. Now ... where was I? ... oh, yes ... you see, we usually just get women with

their children so it would have been good to get the man's point of view ... oh, boys! Please don't make so much noise ... I can't think ... yes, go to your room, please ... there ... *(lifts upstage crate for actor to climb under)* ... thank-you. I have seven children, but ... now, what can I do for you? ... oh, yes ... do you know what I'm going to do?? I am going to get you a lamp, you'd like that, wouldn't you ... yes ... no, you can't come with me it's in the attic and it's very dirty. You go and help Rosemary with the dishes ... I'll be right back ... now where is it? *(climbs under second upstage crate)*
Oh ... yes.

Utter stillness for beginning of WINTER SCENE *immediately following.*

'... do you know what I'm going to do? I am going to get you a lamp, you'd like that, wouldn'd you ... yes ... no.' *Anne*

Act I, Scene IV. Winter Scene.

Actress playing winter enters and covers both crates with a large white sheet. She stands quiet a second and begins 'Winter Poem' before the audience is aware that 'Round the Bend' is finished.

> *Verse one:*
> The middle of winter.
> Inside, everything is cosy and warm, and small.

WINDOW: *(Mime window)*

FROST: *(Blows on the frosted window three times to make a hole to look outside)*

ICICLES: *(Mime shape of icicles dripping, with icicle sound)*

SNOW: *(Wind and snow created from blowing sound and by flapping the sheet around like snow)*

VOICE CODE FOR
FEMALE SPEAKER:
1. *Wife/Mother/Jane*
2. *First Boy (Youngest)*
3. *Second Boy*
   (Older, perhaps Michael)
4. *Neighbour Woman*
5. *Susan (Oldest Child)*
6. *Joan, another neighbour woman*

VOICE CODE FOR
MALE SPEAKER:
1. *Husband/Father/John*
2. *Michael (Older Son)*
3. *Radio*
4. *First Boy (Perhaps*
   Michael's Younger Brother)
5. *Jim, the Bartender*
6. *Herb, The Neighbour*
7. *Dance Caller*

Each actor creates voices and sounds appropriate to the different speakers and situations. Frequent overlap is not dictated by the content of the speeches so much as by the movement of the actors as they tunnel through their separate days and by the feel the two actors develop for each other's presence and rhythms.

1 Rrrring! *(alarm clock)* Up
you get! Oh, John, just look
at that blizzard.

1 Uhh? Didn't *think* it was
going to let up ... using
the car today?

2 Mummy? Can I get up now?
1 All right, come on
downstairs.
You can help me with
the orange juice.

Michael, get up. You've got
to plow out the drive.
2 Right now? Aw Dad ...
1 Jane? Have you seen my
underwear?

Top drawer!

1 Here's the opener.
2 I can ... I can do it.

1 Be sure to call that oil man ...
check the furnace.
1 Mike! Get up now.

1 Do you want some coffee
before you go John?

1 No I'll be back for breakfast
in an hour or so.

3 Hey Mom! Where are my
hockey skates?
1 Under the bed. You can't
sleep with them you know.
2 Mom, can I open the new
Muffets?
3 Aw, *he* got that last time,
Yeah, but you've got *eight*
Mahovaliches and I got
only three.

*Leaves crate 'house', struggles
across stage to 'barn'. Sound
of cattle, waking farm animals.*

1 Get *over*, Elizabeth!
Move over now.

*Milking machine, mooing,
little pigs, radio, etc.*

1 Here's your eggs. Now, eat
up. You're supposed to trade
those cards aren't you?
3 Aw ... I can't eat those.
1 Well you'll need your strength
for the game. Come on, boys.
Put on an extra sweater.
2 Mummy? Can I come with you?
1 No, dear. Susan will be up
soon and she'll play with you.

3 'And now for the weather:
A cold front moving in a
northeasterly direction over
Moosonee ...' etc.
Leaves 'barn', returns to 'house'

Come on, boys.
When we leave, hold on to
my hands. You can't see a foot in
front of your face.
*Leaves crate 'house' and climbs into
shopping cart 'car'*

1 Going to have to do that drive
again before the day's out.
Coffee ...

1 Susan? That bacon ready?

Wife sitting in shopping cart 'car', husband under crate 'house'

Verse two:
Mountains of snow
Block the driveway, ridge the roads.
Map the landscape.
Arms stretched to the sides, steady stare ahead

FEMALE SPEAKER
*Starts 'car' and pushes it along
to bean dryer 'arena' with
appropriate noises.*

MALE SPEAKER
1 Don't take Judy out in this
weather ... bundled up or not
... remember the guy who got
lost between his house
and the barn?

3 Aren't you going to watch?
1 Not to-day. If the storm lets
up, come over to Mrs Tindles'.
It's just a block away
you know. Good luck.
Bye.

4 Daddy? Can I go with you?
1 No, I'm going over to the
other barn ...
1 I'll take the snowmobile ...
be back around five.

*'Car' goes to Mrs Tindles'.
Wife gets out and climbs under
Mrs Tindles' crate 'house'.*

*Leaves 'house', drives old mailbox
'snowmobile' to other 'barn'
making sounds for snowmobile
and then little pigs,
feeding noises, etc.*

1 Hi Gloria.
4 Good heavens, you
made it out.
1 Better take ten dozen.
You never know when
I might not be able
to make it out again.
4 Did you hear about
the Gelling's baby ...
blue.

1 Heavens, yes. Got
a card from them
asking for a prayer.
4 Well, I don't know
what good my
prayers will do.
1 Well they've got a
good family anyway.
A girl and two boys.
1 Uh, huh. Oh here's
the boys, better be off.

2 Can we stay inside
for a minute?
1 No, come on now;
get into the car. See you
later Gloria. Thanks for
the coffee.
4 Take it easy now.
3 Mom. You know
what he did?
He let in eight goals.
2 You didn't *see* that ...
1 No fighting. Now get
into the back seat.

*'Car' returns home, wife climbs
under crate 'house'.*

2 Boy, I'm going to build a
snow fort!
1 No you're not. In you get. Oh
Susan, did you get the coffee
urn up from the basement?
5 Yeah ... it's on the table.
5 I put the roast in the oven.
1 Oh, good, honey. Thanks.
1 You'll see that the dinner gets
on will you? I've got to go
early to the square dancing

*Leaves other 'barn', snowmobiles
to 'bar' in town.*

5 Close that *door*!
1 Let me *in* first ... have two
beers Jim.
5 Hear McFarlane's workin for
Taylor now ...
6 Show him what a day's work
is, heh, heh.
5 Used to be preem-yeer of the
country ...
6 I'm a city man myself ...
1 Now she's a *good woman* ...
5 Ever been out of work before
(laughter of various kinds)
1 Wife's got plans for the dance
tonight ... yah ... not me,
I guess.
5 Close that *door*!

*Leaves 'bar', snowmobiles to bean
dryer 'arena', parks, climbs under.
Or, if there's time, goes back home
first, talks to the kids, puts on tie,
etc. Obviously the two actors have
to work out their own timing so
they arrive at the 'arena' for
the appropriate mesh of
dialogue just before Freeze 3.
(for example:)*

1 Where's your mother? Oh.
Did you see my red tie
anywhere, Susan? No, you
can't go over to Billie's. You
saw him yesterday. Once
a week is enough. Never see

36

'Mountains of snow
Block the driveway, ridge the roads.
Map the landscape.'
Janet and David

to-night with refreshments.

5 Yeah.

2 Mommie, see what I did?

1 Oh *that's* lovely. Why don't
   you put it on your wall?
   Now is that everything?

1 Bye now.

1 Oh, a new dress.

6 That's something, eh?
   I picked the material up in
   Goderich last summer and
   finally got around to it.

6 Say, where's the men?

1 Well, I can tell you where
   John was. Oh here he comes.

your mother from morning
to night some days. Going to
the dance. Be back by
midnight. Yah. O.K.
Don't touch the furnace.

1 Good to see you, Harold ...
   You know women, ... always
   get the best of the bargain.

1 Where's Janie?

*Both wife and husband huddle out of sight under the bean dryer
'arena'.*

Verse three:
STILL:

QUIET: *(pause)*

STARS: *(make three stars with hands and sound)*

THE SNOW
CREAKS WHEN YOU WALK ON IT. *(three squeaking sounds making
foot prints with hands)*

SQUARE DANCE CALL
*Bean dryer bounces in time, sounds of dancing, applause, fatigue,
etc., from the 'crowd' in the 'arena'.*

Now, on to your partners!
Now, corners address.
Now all join hands, and circle left!
Circle left, go round the ring
Around the ring with a pretty wee thing,
Now break and swing!
Now, first couple! Up to the right!
And dip and dive across the floor,
Go in again out again in again

Once again!
All the way there,
And all the way back!

FEMALE SPEAKER	MALE SPEAKER
1 Ohhh! Hey.	
1 I must have lost ten pounds on that one.	1 I'm gonna buy some heifers from him.
6 Come over sometime.	1 Herb, get away from that bar.
1 I'll give you a call tomorrow. O.K.	1 Janie, are you coming? It's after midnight.

Both leave the 'arena', pause, look at the stars

1 Stopped.

1 That's a blessing.

1 Watch that corner, it's treacherous.

Into their respective vehicles and drive home with appropriate noises

1 I'll hold that door for you.

1 Susan? Are you still up?
5 Yeah ... watching the late movie.

1 Well, get to bed as soon as the show's over.
1 Well, there was no stopping *you* tonight, you must have danced every dance.

1 Well, I should *say*!
1 Move *over*, you lug!

1 I was just trying to get *warm*.

Both actors back in their original crates

Verse four:
THE MOON: (*mime moon with hands*)
Bright.
THE SNOW: (*look straight ahead, stretch both arms straight in front, and slowly spread them to the sides*)
Stretches, for miles.

Act I, Scene v. Bale Scene.

Actor enters carrying a straw bale, sets it down. When he begins to speak, WINTER SCENE *actors break from their* FREEZE, *and with help from other actors carry off their crates or whatever, and exit. Their casual, deliberate movements should suggest a purpose other than simply moving props so that the audience, like the newly-arrived 'Farm-hand', is watching men working at a job which looks simple but is at first slightly incomprehensible.*

As part of the preparation for this play, we wanted to go around to some of the different farmers and see if we could help with the work. So one afternoon me and another fellow had the opportunity to help Mr Mervin Lobb with his haying.

Well when we got there, they had this big old-fashioned wagon outside the barn, loaded up with bales. And next to it was this metal chute thing which I found out they called the outside loader, and that went up to the top of the barn to what they called the mow.

Now there were already five people working there and we made seven, so we asked Mr Lobb if he thought he could keep seven of us busy up in the mow. He said, 'Nooo ...,' he thought I should stay down there and help him. So the other fellows climbed up the loader into the mow, and I stayed down below to see what would happen.

Mr Lobb climbed down off the wagon and picked up this plug and socket thing ... and he plugged her in. Rrr-Rrr Rrr! *(makes sound of bale elevator)* Then he climbed back on the wagon and he picked up a bale, and he put it on the edge of the wagon. Well, I looked at the bale and I looked at the loader, and I put two and two together ... *(Mime of lifting, loading, carrying, etc. of bales begins and continues to the end of the scene as the actor recreates the experience.)* So I picked up the bale, and put it on the loader ... Look out! *(apologetically)* Fell off ... Well, I picked up, and put it on the loader, pressed it down, and up she went! ... oh, yeah, ... another one. Well it was right about this time that I figured out one thing. I wasn't dressed for it. You see, all I had on was a little pair of shorts, and the only way I could get the bale up onto the loader was by *pushing* it along with my leg, which was getting pretty cut up, and sore. Well, it was pretty hot that day ... about eighty-five, and we working along at what I figgered was a pretty good pace – look out! *(bales come crashing down)*

Well, I was having a little trouble keeping the bales on the loader. But after awhile I figgered out how to get the bales unto the loader, press them down, and ... moving along ... Look at *that*, Mr Lobb! Three in a row! ... oh. Yes, sir. Well, after what seemed an awfully long time in the hot sun, we got that load off the wagon, unto the loader, and up ... into ... the mow.

Then I discovered one of the greatest things in the world. Freshie!

Right about this time a bunch of the fellows up in the mow had to go off to the fields to make up another load, so they said I probably ought to go up *there* and help. Which was o.k. with me, 'cause any job had to be better than the one I was doing! So I climbed up unto the loader which they'd turned off, and climbed up ... into ... the mow. *(coughing)* Well, it was kind of dusty ... and hot, and it had these wooden sloping rafters that came all the way down to the floor. The floor was nothing but these bales which had been piled up. Well, there were three of us up there; myself, the fella who had come with me, and Tom, who worked there. Well, I didn't know what to do up there either, so I figured I'd just stand there and let them show me. So they plugged her in down below and the first bale came up, and Tom picked her up, carried her over, and put her down. Then the next bale came up, the other fella picked her up, carried her over, and put her down. Oh, my turn. So I went over ... up she came, I grabbed hold – broke. (Well I'll just kick it over the edge here.) Up came the next one. I picked it up, carried her over ... and ... put ... it ... down. Whew! Huh? Oh, it's my turn again. Well, I went back and it was right about then that I discovered something they *have* up in these mows. *(falls hard)*

They've got *holes*! They've got lots of holes. Well, I got up, picked up the bale and carried it over, and came back, tripping over the baling twine, falling in the holes. I was a mess.

Well, then they took pity on me. 'Why don't you be the feeder?' they said. I didn't know what that was either, so they showed me. The feeder is the guy who just stands there. The bale comes up. And he *heaves* it into the corner! Well, I went over. Up came the bale, I grabbed a hold of it, and *heaved* it into the corner! *(falling in the process)* Not quite as far as the other fella's, but I was working on it. Well, right away, I discovered a couple of disadvantages to *this* job. Instead of handling every third bale, you had to heave every bale. And the only way I could get any distance on these bales was by pushing them along with my leg. Which was getting pretty cut up ... It was pretty hot up in the mow. It was about 135 degrees and rising, and the baling twine was beginning to raise blisters the size of balloons on my hands, and – itchy!

Now the fella that had come with me, he *loved* this kind of stuff,

'I'd go back, grab another one, *heave!* grab another one! *Heave! Miles*

he'd pick up a bale, put it over his head a couple of times, 'It's *good* for you boy, you're going home skinny today!' Tom, the fella who worked there, he'd just pick it up, carry it over, and set it down. I'd go back, grab another one, *heave*! grab another one! *Heave*! And, finally. After what seemed like forever! There it was. The last bale. *(Bales have been getting heavier. This one is heaved with great effort.)* I went ... and stood in the entrance to the mow. I let the breeze blow over my body ..., and dry the sweat ..., and the blood. *(Pause)* Then I looked *down* ... and they were bringing up *another wagon*! He gets off, and plugs her in! This time I wasn't even the feeder. It was every man for himself!

Well, I grabbed the first bale ... carried it over ... went back for another one. By this time every muscle and bone in my body was screaming 'Go home, go home!'.

But I said, 'No, by God, I ain't a quitter, I'm gonna see this through to the bitter end!'

But, finally I said, 'Oh, the hell with it! I'm gonna start rolling them.' Have you ever tried rolling a square bale? I rooolled it ... and I went back for another one ... and I rooolled it over ... and finally! Up it came. The last bale of the day! *(Pause. Wait for it.)* Come on, you son-of-a ... bitch.

(Lifts, and carries it over with great effort, finishing the last few feet on his knees. Walks over and sits on the real bale he carried in at the beginning of the scene, exhausted) Now, I ask you ... why!? Why would any human being *choose*, for the better part of his life, *twice* a year, to put himself through that total and utter hell? I didn't understand it then ... and I don't understand it now. *(exit)*

Act I, Scene VI. Les Jervis.

> FIRST GIRL
> *(enters stage left and mimes while speaking)*

A tall, wire fence – bent.
Thick fence posts,
Enclose a smooth, flat pond.
A water-wheel,
Turning.
Above it,
A sign written in black.
Time.

> *(sits centre stage with hands like two ducks' heads)*

Ducks!
Swimming on the pond.

> SECOND GIRL
> *(enters stage right and mimes while speaking)*

A sparsely wooded hill,
Sloping down
Into a clay bank,
And into the water.
Trees.
Deer,
Small, with white spots.
Staring.

> LES JERVIS

(enters carrying pail) What d'you *call* these places that you go into ...?
When you're travelling around, and you're going to stop over ...
eyeah ... Information Bureaus!
   Well, anyway, they had this card with my duck-pond,
don't-you-see ... well, I call it my duck-pond. They call it my
sanctuary. Well, anyways, I couldn't understand why all these
Americans were coming through, but they'd look up this card and see
about this sanctuary, and they used to come around ... just wait. I
gotta spit.

Fina and her ducks

AMERICAN TOURIST LADY
(enters stage left)
Fluffy white ducks!
Peacocks.
And a sign that says, 'Please feed us grass.
Grampa's too old to bend down.'
Actress now gradually becomes a peacock.

LES JERVIS
I feed my deers the very best of alfalfa hay. I don't feed corn. I feed
oats and barley. It's the same with the sheep. Oh, but if the
government does anything to get their hands on them – this fellow
told me the other day, he said, 'Now that you've got this place set up,
don't you go puttin' any Canadian deers in here. 'Cause sure as you
do, some young fella'll come round here with his chest stickin' out and
tell you got to be feedin' them timothy hay, or you have to this, or you
have to do that.' And he said, 'You stick to European deers, and the
government doesn't have anything to do with it.' And that's the best
way to have it. He's a good friend of mine. I've got whitedeer on the
other side. They call them English Fallow deer. I see the young
fellow's followin' the pair of old ones around now. Ohh you know ...
people 'ud steal the Lord's supper nowadays. I had two wonderful ...
uh ... oh ... pheasants, y'know, different breeds? Chinese pheasants,
an', an', ... well, I came down here one day an' the *hen* bird was gone.
Well ... somebody wanted one, don't y'see, an' came in here and
helped themselves ... so ... I don't know.
Actor enters as ram stage right.
Now that's an old black Persian ram, 'n' he's a mean old bugger and
I'm deaf, so I put this old cow bell on 'im. Uh ... he won't hurt you so
long as you're *lookin'* at 'im, but as soon as you turn away, why that's
when he'd ... uh ... give you the works! So I put this old cow bell on
him, 'n' now, soon as he starts gettin' up and starts comin' at you, why
I can just step aside and let him go by then ... ('Course, if he ever hit a
fella, he'd break your hip, y'know). Ahh, but then *feedin'*'s quite a
problem, 'n' there's only one fellow I know, if I took sick, there's only
one fellow I know could come by – 'n' he's nearly as old as I am, an'
know where things is around. *(sits)* I got the *idea* for my duck pond
when we was over in West Germany on one of old Hitler's autobahns?
Visitin' my son Ivan ... in Fontainbleau, France ... N.A.T.O.
Headquarters ... Oh, I been all over Canada visitin', I've been up the
Alaska Highway, I've been everywheres ...
Anyways, I said to my wife ... and this was when they didn't have
jets then either. They had these here Eng ... no ... what d'you call

46

them? Oh ... roy ... Royal Royce engines on them, way out on the sides? Well, I said to my wife, I said, 'I'm goin' over to see *Ivan*!' Well, my other boys all laughed, thought it was a hell of a joke. Anyways, I got on this baby and away we went! An', d'you know? The hum of them motors was in my ears for two days after? Oh, an' we hit a storm! Near scared the shit outta me ...'bout half way over.

It was a son-of-a-bitch of a jump in the air, an' ... an' then we came down 'bout so far ... right in about the middle. Well, anyways, it scared me. 'N' before, *after* we started, they give us how to use this, uh, this belt that goes around your middle, and then there's the one they give you if you're gonna take to the water, 'n' all this here. An' o'course I'm dull of hearin'... *Anyway*, we made the buck jump in the air and then came back down ... and then *she* came in hollerin', an' I thought she said, uh, oh, what d'you call them? ... life jackets! So I said, 'Listen, I'm not gonna be *all* day.' So I up 'n' grabbed the damn jacket, jerked it down, an' a *Frenchman* sittin' beside me said, 'No, no, no, no, no', he said. Well, 'n' it was the belt around *your* middle they wanted you to do up. Well, I said, 'I'm not gonna swim home! I used to be a bugger to swim, but I'm not gonna swim home!'

Well, anyways we got over there, and we went through *eight* countries. And Hitler's autobahn! We was drivin' along side of the Alps, an' we looked away down at this little village with all these cars. And Ivan said – that's my son – he said, 'We'll just go down there and see what's goin' on.' Well, by golly, we did. 'N' trust a German, he was makin' money! He had a gas pump on one side, and an eatin' house on the other, and the tourists was payin' him money. He had, uh, one o'these oh, what d'y'call them – ohh – they're awful beasts ... *Swans*! *black* swans – white from here up – and German stags for deers. Oh, he had a swanky outfit! Well, I said to Ivan, I said, 'I got a better place than he's got!' 'n' he said, 'Where?' 'N' I said, 'Up the road as you go to Holmesville!' I said. 'I'm gonna build a place just like that when I get back.' Well, he laughed, thought it was a big joke.

But, anyways, I got back here and we was two months diggin', pullin' stumps outta the swamp, puttin' in fence posts. Was I sick of the job! It's a hobby, it's nothin' more than a hobby. It's got nothin' to do with the government!

I used to farm – had horses, cattle, 'n' pigs. Built a nice big barn behind the, uh, the, oh, the *bushes* up there. It had a concrete floor and the stalls was higher than the floor so the pee would run off both sides...

Now that was to the east of the Disney property. That's the Disneys from down south. Now you might catch me on the history of this but oh, two or three generations ago they had a mill on the Maitland, then they moved up to Bluevale, 'n' then on down to the

'I got the *idea* for my duck pond when we was over in West Germany on one of old Hitlers autobahns.' *David as Les Jervis*

States. Well, you know, maybe I shouldn't say this, but that Walt Disney never had a pot to piss in till Mickey Mouse, and that's a fact.

But, then I sold the farm to the, oh ... uh ... the Dutchman. Well anyways, we moved out 'n' the wife forgot somethin', so she sent me back to fetch it, and, of course, I went. And to have to *knock* on your own back door! That fella coulda made a lot of money right then and there – I'd a paid him anything he asked for it! To get it *back*, don't y'see!

> *The first two actors shift position to become a water-wheel and*
> *bridge.*

Now, that's my old water-wheel, 'n' he's just like old Father Time, he just goes on an' on an' on. An', an' the water drives it, if you watch it close you'll see the water fallin' off it. My grandsons helped me build it. They said, 'Time's goin' faster now, so we'd better speeed him up!' Well, time's goin' too fast now, so I'm gonna go back there, an' shut him off, just turn 'im down so he's just goin' over, just turnin' over, and that's all. *(exit)*

Act I, Scene VII. Orange Parade

Confusion and appropriate conversation as actors come onstage representing people gathering for the parade. The parade itself is a solemn walk around the stage representing the Goderich Town Square. Band forms stage right composed of soprano recorder 'fife'. Les Jervis' pail 'drum'. As the band crosses in front of the stage George Walsh advances from centre stage, his arms outstretched.

GEORGE WALSH

My name's George Walsh from Blyth, Ontario. We've been coming to the Orange walk on the Glorious Twelfth of July for twenty years now.

This is the open Bible. It symbolizes the faith of our fore-fathers, living still. *(falls into step behind the band circling the stage)*

WOMAN

L.O.B.A. – Ladies Orange Benevolent Association.

REVEREND CARSON

To emulate his virtue by maintaining religion without persecution, William of Orange was invited to England by the clergy and nobles. He came in 1688, and the people welcomed him.

ROY ROBINSON

This is the sword of office *(arm outstretched)* of the scarlet degree of the Orange Order. I'm Roy Robinson from Briton, Ontario. We won a prize this year for the best dressed group. You can see I have a nice white suit here, and an orange sash – it's a great day for Briton!

REVEREND CARSON

Constitutional Government was established and the Bill of Rights was passed in 1689, and he triumphed. The victorious Battle of the Boyne was fought in 1690. To keep alive the memory of these glorious events, and to act as a bulwark against any aggression, the Orange Association was formed.

MAN

I'm from Kintail, from the Morningstar Lodge, and you'll see on this banner the red figure of a beaver. And crossed over its back are two union jacks. Then, up in each corner are two small maple leaves. Now, that represents Canadian rule, under British justice.

Commotion. Actors break from parade figures to become audience for the following speech.

SPEAKER

Thank-you, Reverend Carson, for those words of wisdom. Now, it's time we got back into those old history books and found out where we *really* had our beginnings. Now we really had our beginnings in a group that was known as St. John's of Jerusalem. Now this was an organisation that was founded at the time of the ... *(checks notes)* the Romans! The Roman Empire was taxin' them to death! So they formed an organisation that was known as St. John's of Jerusalem. And it grew ... and it grew ... and it grew. Until it became what is known today as Orangism! *(mild applause)* And if we lasted that long, we ought to be good for another couple of thousand years!

Applause. Actors resume parade at a slower pace.

WOMAN

Rows of women, dressed in white. White shoes, white dresses, white gloves, and over their right shoulders, white parasols. Thirty members of the Beulah Lodge of Fordwich, Ontario, walk solemnly in formation, following a woman carrying in an open Bible.

Parade trails off backstage.

LODGE MEMBER

Well, now! After the garbage has been all picked up, some of you people won't even *think* about Orangism until next twelfth of July! But we want you to *remember* that we're in the community, and we're *working* for you. And this year, we have set up what is known as the Five Counties Orange League Benevolent Fund. So I'd like to call now on Mrs Bertrand McCreath! *(Whistle blows activating marching band backstage.)* And Roger Wilkinson ... no, Roger's on holidays. What's that fellow's name ... Roger Bushland! To come forward and accept this donation on *behalf* of the Five Counties Orange League Benevolent Fund to the Boy Scouts of Goderich, Ontario! *(cut off by marching band which has by now advanced up stage right and crossing to stage left)*

YOUNG CONQUEROR
(Last member of marching band mimes dramatic cymbal crash and turns to address the audience while the rest of the band proceeds in its circle backstage.)

James Johnson! Young Conqueror! London, Ontario. We come down here every year. They give us a bus. It gives us some practice. And it helps the old fellows out with their parade, if you know what I mean. Oops! They're coming around again!

Band has by this time completed its circle and is coming up stage right again playing 'My Bonnie Lassie' or whatever so that the cymbal player now becomes its leader.

BOB MCKINLEY
(One of the band members left backstage during the last circle now advances to centre stage, warmly greeted and escorted by the lodge member who has been nervously lingering there during the Young Conqueror speech.)
Ladies and Gentlemen. *(All freeze.)* I would like to thank you very, very much for inviting me here to help you celebrate the Glorious Twelfth of July Walk. Some of you may not know this, but for my wife Audrey and me, this is a *double* celebration. You see, it's our twenty-third Wedding Anniversary.
Marchers break from their freeze, crowd around with appropriate exclamations.
And I can't think of a way I'd rather celebrate it than to be here with you on this beautiful tree-lined square in the county seat of Goderich.
Mild cheers, applause. Parade resumes.

LODGE MEMBER
Thank-you, Mr McKinley. Thank you very much. *(shakes his hand vigorously)* We want you to remember that Mr McKinley is the Member of Parliament for this region, and we're very *proud* to have ... *(cut off by True Blue, exits backstage with McKinley)*

TRUE BLUE
Banner!
Loyal Orange Lodge Number Seven Oh One.
Faith of our fathers.
They suffered death rather than submit to Popism.
We have here the Boys of Derry, and some monks kneeling, with a crucifix before them.

GRAND MARSHALL
(Actor miming a man riding a frisky and unruly horse)
King William of Orange! On a white horse. Grand Marshall, Loyal Orange Lodge, Goderich.

Parade continues with fewer people at a slower pace.

SPEAKER

Well, now, I'd like to tell you one of those Newfie jokes. I don't think
there's any harm in telling them, everyone's telling them nowadays.
Anyway there was this Newfie, you see, and he went in to buy a used
car. So he went in there and he's looking around, and the fellow says to
him … well, I don't know what the fellow says to him … I wasn't
there. But he picks out the car, and *then* the fellow says to him, 'Well
all right, Newfie – but that car don't have any reverse gear.' And then
the Newfie says, 'Oh that's all right I'm not coming back this way
anyway!'

MRS BERTRAND MCCREATH

On behalf *(All freeze)* of the Girl Guides, Brownies, and Rangers, we
certainly do appreciate, and thank you very, very kindly for this
generous donation. Thank-you very much. *(Break freeze)*

SPEAKER

See, the Newfie thought …

LITTLE GIRL

(very excited) I've decorated the wheels of my tricycle with orange and
blue streamers going all the way around! And my mother made me a
new orange dress! And I put orange ribbons in my hair, and I'm in the
parade to-day!

CLARK JOHNSON

(enters from backstage a little drunk, enjoying himself immensely) Well I'm
going to sing one more song. And then I'm going home!

LITTLE GIRL

Why?

CLARK JOHNSON

Gotta milk the cows.

OLD CRONY

(setting him up) You got no milking machine, Clark?

CLARK JOHNSON

(playing back to him) No, I use the two on four method! *(Both start to
laugh)*

LITTLE GIRL
(innocently) What's that?

CLARK JOHNSON
That? Oh that. Well, you put two hands on the ... front and two
hands on the ... *(sees he's losing his audience)* I've got to sing the *song*! It's
called, 'The Laughing Song.'

LAUGHING SONG
Verse one:
Well I'm tickled in the morning, and I'm tickled at night,
And I'm tickled everywhere about the whole world.
Well my wife she tickles in the middle of the afternoon,
And I'm tickled everywhere I go.
And it's ah ha ha ha ha ha ha ha ha ha ha,
He he he he he ha ha ha ha ha ha ha ha
Ha ha ha ha ha ha ha ha ha ha
Well something's always sure to tickle me.

Verse two:
And now I put some pepper in my dad's snuff box,
Oh great delight it was a sight to see-ee,
Well he coughed and he choked and spit
Till I thought he'd take a fit
And then he up and *he* tickled *me*
And it's ah ha ha ha ha ha ha ha ha ha ha
Oh ha ha ha ha ha ha ha ha ha ha ha
Ha ha ha ha ha ha ha ha ha ha
Well something's always sure to tickle meeeeee-ee-ee!

clapping and cheers from the audience

Thank you. Thank you very kindly, folks. If I ever make it back to the
next Twelfth I'll be sure to sing ... *(exit cut off by Clergyman)*

CLERGYMAN
I think the answer is to be found in that well-known Protestant hymn,
'Protestant Boys' in the fourth stanza:
      And long may the fame of their glory remain,
      Unclouded by age and undimmed by stain.
      And ever and ever the cause we'll uphold
      The cause of the true and the trusted, and bold,
      And scorn to yield or leave the field,

'Well my wife she tickles in the middle of the afternoon. And I'm tickled everywhere I go.' *Paul as Clark*

While over our heads the banners shall play,
And traitors shall tremble wherever we assemble,
For Protestant boys shall carry the day.

SPEAKER

Ladies and Gentlemen, it's not over yet, ohh no! It's only begun!
There'll be a concert and a street dance tonight behind McGee's
Garage. We hope to have you all back here with us at that time. And
now, on *behalf* of the Goderich Orange Lodge, I'd like to thank all
those who attended and made this day the wonderful success that it's
been. I thank you very much.

MAN

(walking slowly, reading a newspaper) I'm reading from the Goderich
Signal-Star, and this fellow writes:
'It appears that much of the glory has gone out of the Twelfth of July
Celebration. Well, perhaps it has. Tom Deeve from the Murphy
Lodge in Clinton was telling me that ten years ago there used to be
two hundred and fifty members. Today there are no more than
forty-five. But, you see. We, in the Orange Lodge believe in, and
practise, good works. We believe that these are troubled times, and
that the answer is to be found in the open book, in the open Bible, if
we can only decipher it. But this fellow goes on: 'On Saturday,
merchants around the square suffered a day-long dollar-drought to
perpetuate a fast-fading tradition.'
You see, *if* the glory is going out, it's not the fault of the Orange
Lodge. It's the fault of all those who put the *dollar* before they put
anything else. *(exit)*

Act I, Scene VIII. Charlie Wilson.

One actor plays Charlie Wilson consistently. Other members of the cast are visible but this scene is largely a voice portrait drawn from the memories of people who knew him.

JANET
Last summer we asked one of the farmers if he knew anyone in the area who was considered eccentric. Someone who was a bit strange and outside of the community. He said the only man he could think of was a man named Charlie Wilson.

MAN
Well, I can tell you one thing about Charlie Wilson – he's dead.

JANET
Well, we went around and asked people what they remembered about Charlie.

WOMAN
Charlie had two shacks that he lived in, one for the summer and one for the winter. His winter shack would be, oh, about this *(paces it off)* long and about that wide. He had a bed, a wood stove, and a table. He didn't have a chair, he would pull the table up to the bed and he had some boxes for his books and his groceries.

CHARLIE
(reading from letter) 'Mr J.E. Little, South Street, Goderich. Hello, Ern. I received the parcel you sent me last Christmas'.

WOMAN
He had what, I guess you'd call a tic, on the side of his face, and he'd work it and rub it and his tongue would roll out the side of his mouth, so it was very difficult to understand what he was saying. Oh, I didn't know him very well. Alma used to ...

MAN
You could always tell one of Charlie's tools. He would go out and find a discarded head of a shovel, or an adze, and if he couldn't find a handle, he would go out in the brush and cut a limb, and then just carve it down till it fit. Then he would go out and find all kinds of nuts and bolts and wire things and then put them together. Well, it looked funny, but it worked.

'My tic, my tic dally roo, bothers me so much sometimes that I can't get to sleep.' *David as Charlie*

MAN

He was a lonely man. He spent a lot of time just by himself. But he used to come over to our house every Thursday night exactly at 6:00 for supper and then he'd watch *Bonanza*. I was one of the few people who ever saw the inside of his shack.

CHARLIE

'The severity of my tic prevented me acknowledging receipt before this. Dante's Divine Comedy contains some interesting historical notes, such as that purgatory was introduced to the Papal form of Christianity in the 6th Century by Pope Gregory.'

WOMAN

I can tell you exactly what Charlie looked like. He had a long lean face that looked like it was hewn out of white elm. He was very pale and he had a square jaw and his chin stuck out just a little. He was always clean-shaven, but occasionally you could see his beard, and it would be white.

MAN

Charlie? Oh, Charlie was a corker, he'd get off some good ones – I remember once he started in ...

WOMAN

He was one of the best educated men I knew – and he was self-educated. He used to come over to play cards with Fred. He wouldn't stay for dinner because he was ashamed of his tic. I knew him for fifty-three years.

CHARLIE

(moves to different spot onstage) Now, that's Brassica Oleracia. *You'd* call it wild cabbage. You can tell by the waxy texture of the leaves. Now, that's a young plant. Some of them grow one – two feet high. The waxy texture of the leaves protects them from freezing in a temperate climate.

WOMAN

He would always wear a clean, blue shirt, and when you passed by his two shacks, you would see hanging out on the line, between them; a pair of blue striped overalls and a blue shirt. Now in summer he wore a rail-roader's hat, and in winter he had sort of a fur cap. *(Charlie moves back into 'shack')*

MAN

Work? Oh yeah, Charlie worked, and he had a pension and a bit of land. But most of the time he did odd jobs. Now if you hired Charlie for an odd job, he'd be by at nine in the morning, wanting to know what's to be done and he'd start in doing it. Then at twelve noon, he'd quit and be gone till one. Then he'd be back and he'd work until five o'clock or until the job was done. But I tell you, don't get Charlie talking, 'cause if you get him talking you wouldn't get a thing done. Now I remember once he was talking to me ...

WOMAN

Women and the Bible! Charlie didn't have any use for either of them. The things he used to say would curl your hair.

MAN

In the middle of winter he used to walk the mile or so to our place and when he'd get inside, he'd sit almost as if he was in a trance for half an hour, and then he'd rub his cheek. The kids were kind of repulsed by that.

CHARLIE

My tic, my tic *dally roo*, bothers me so much sometimes that I can't get to sleep. I often think I would like to go down to the Maitland and chop a hole in the ice and jump in. But with my luck *(laughing tone)* the axe handle would probably break.

WOMAN

Well, he chewed tobacco and he took snuff and the smell of his pipe was enough to knock an elephant over.

MAN

Oh, you could argue with Charlie, but he didn't have any sense of ... ah ... humour!

WOMAN

Charlie Wilson had a wonderful wit! Now that Les Jervis, well everyone knows he's full of it.

MAN

I remember when old Bert Lobb went to visit him in the hospital, Charlie had cancer and he showed Bert his open sore. Well, Bert was so mad at those doctors for keeping him alive and in pain he nearly took the roof off that hospital.

MAN
He was odd and kept apart, but he's in heaven!

CHARLIE
'Wishing you the compliments of the season and again thanking you for your kindness, I remain, your friend, Charlie Wilson … Address, J. Chas. Wilson, RR2, Clinton Ontario. *(exit)*

Act I, Scene IX. Man on a Tractor.

Three actors standing in a row form a tractor with appropriate
sounds. Man mounted on middle actor's shoulders steers.

MAN

Now the thing about a farmer and his tractor is that he's gotta spend so
much time on it. If I had a dollar for every hour I've spent on this thing
... whew! I wouldn't have to be on this thing! It's like my friend Bill
Lobb used to say ... sometimes a man gets to taking better care of his
tractor than he does his wife! Haw, haw. But, you know, depending
on what you're cropping, you may have to go over the *same* area, five,
six, seven times in one season, and that can be pretty boring. But you
can't let the boredom *get* to you. No, you gotta be awake, you gotta be
alert, you gotta be watching. Say you're scuffling beans, for example,
– well you gotta be looking *behind* you, to see that you're not tearing
out those rows of beans that you planted, or you're discing. You gotta
watch that the earth's not piling up between those discs and slowing
you down. And you gotta listen to the sound of that motor, 'cause you
don't want it to be lugging, you want it to do the job you paid for that
tractor to do. And there's always a bit of danger involved. I don't
know anybody on this line hasn't turned his tractor or come pretty
near to it one time or another. Now you can see, I got a bugger of a hill
right over there – every time I go up there, I think well, this could be
it! It's a steep hill, loose earth, and a heavy tractor. It could just flip
over and come crashing down! But you can't *think* about that. It's all
part of being a farmer – it's all part of being a tractor! *(exit)*

'sometimes a man gets to taking better care of his tractor than he does his wife!' *Anne, Paul, Miles, Fina*

Act I, Scene X. Washing Woman.

Woman appears pushing washing machine to centre stage, or, if no wheels, she gets her husband to help.

MARION

You know, if you'd get that thing fixed, we wouldn't have to carry it out here every time. *(to audience)* I was *so* busy yesterday, I had so much to do that when I woke up this morning I had a headache and I had to take an aspirin. Well, I feel better now, but I've decided to take it easy to-day. I'm going to stay right here in this house *(climbs into washing machine and squats down)* and maybe do a little housework.

If there's one thing you've got to have on a farm, it's your *health*. If you're not healthy, you're no good to anyone. *(begins dusting machine)* Oh, just look at that.

I'll just give you an idea of what I did yesterday. I started out at five thirty and collected my eggs. Well I do that every morning. You see, I have five hundred new pullets, year-old chickens, and I'm the only one who can collect the eggs because they get very excited ... *(Jim's speech below overlaps last sentence.)*

JIM

Marion! Marion, I have to go to the dealers. I'll be back about one-thirty ...

MARION

What? What did you say, dear?

JIM

I said I have to go down to the dealers for shear-pins. I'll be back about one or one-thirty. So if we could have dinner ...

MARION

But I took you in yesterday!

JIM

I know. But they shear off in tough hay. We'll need you out on the tractor about three. So, if you could ...

MARION

No! I'm not going out of this house today. I need a rest.

'I'm going to stay right here in this house and maybe do a little housework.'
Janet as Washing Woman

JIM

Well, you're the only one left, so I'll see you on the tractor at three ...
(exit)

MARION

Well, maybe Jane could help you! That girl never does a thing around
here! Maybe she could ... Oh well, I must remember to speak to Jane.
Then I made breakfast as usual but I didn't have a chance to do the
dishes because I had to take the boys to their hockey practice. They
have hockey practice on Tuesdays and Saturdays and baseball
practice on, uh, let me see, Thursdays, yes, but Elizabeth takes them
on Thursdays, so that's all right. Then I decided to do my grocery
shopping at the same time and kill two birds with one stone after I
dropped Jim off at the implement dealers, but I forgot my list.
Wouldn't you know! And I forgot the cheese. Well, I was ...

BOY

(enters with old cap advertising Funk's corn) Mom ...? Mom ...? Mom?
(finally gets her attention)

MARION

What is it dear? *(to audience)* Excuse me.

BOY

Mom, would you wash my Funk's hat please? Thank you.

MARION

Just a *minute*! You come here! Now I've told you *three* times to get rid
of this filthy old thing. If I see it again, I'll *burn* it!

BOY

(whining) Aw, come on, Mom. It's my lucky Funk's hat. I gotta have it.
If I don't have it, we'll lose the game!

MARION

I'm not washing it. No son of mine is going to be seen wearing a hat
like that!

BOY

Pleeeeeeeease?

MARION

(sighs) Oh, all right. But this is the *last time*!

66

BOY

Thanks Mom. I knew it. *(Kisses her)* I love you! *(exit)*

MARION

Excuse me, I'll just start the washing. Oh, yes. Well, I was having some ladies in and wouldn't you know it the one thing that Mrs Hislop loves is cheese?

JANE

(enters carrying laundry) Would you wash this please? I'm going to the dance to-night. Thank-you. *(exit)*

MARION

Jane? Jane! Your father wants you on the tractor at three o'clock. *(overlays Jane's speech above)* And don't you talk to me like that young lady or you'll get no ... *(sigh)* Excuse me while I get this laundry in. *(starts to gyrate)* Well, I had to go back and get some cheese and by the time I go back at eleven thirty the eggs were all over the place.

MARY

(enters carrying bag) Mom this isn't garbage!
Knock on door off stage

MARION

I've put it out three times. Could you answer the door please? I thought that you ... The pullets you see, don't know how to lay in the nests yet. And then I had to get the boys ... *(phone rings)* Hello? Oh, hello Elizabeth. No, I thought you were ...

MAN

(enters with Mary) Feed man! Could you sign here ma'am.

MARY

You're new around here, aren't you?
knock on door offstage

MARION

Do you have a pencil? My husband is out in the barn. *(to Elizabeth on the phone)* I can't pick up the boys. I have to take it easy today.

WOMAN

(enters with basket) I've come for my eggs! I ordered three dozen this morning.

MARION

Mary, try and find a pencil. *(to audience)* Then the card party arrived and I hadn't time to do the dishes all day. *(to egg woman)* Well, I'm sorry, the bakery has bought all the eggs.

MAN

(to Mary) No, I don't have a pencil. *(to Marion)* Your husband isn't out in the barn. I've gone out there for the last ...

Boy enters holding a hurt thumb, gets into an argument with his sister and chases her around washer, woman and feed man wait impatiently, Marion's speech has been gradually speeding up until now, gyrating furiously, she is incomprehensible. Other actors draw back into position for square dance. With a loud squawk and flap, Marion turns into a chicken.

JIM

(pause) What's for dinner!

MARION

(sung to the tune of 'Turkey in the Straw' while square dance is performed around her using imaginary as well as real partners to fill out the set)

Verse one:

Oh, a teachin' woman came to Clinton town.
Maisy sang in the choir but was lookin' up and down.
For a man she could love who would care for her.
She found him in the kitchen with a can opener.
He was fat and greasy, drank like a fish.
He could cook up a storm and he was a dish,
But he yearned for a farm and to have a spouse,
To do those dishes and be quiet as a mouse.

WOMAN

(advances to stage front) Well, I never minded doing the washing, not since I got my new Maytag. Front loader! *(claps her dance partner on the back so that he bends over forming a washer)* I just stuff the clothes in here like this, close the door, and give it a good kick! *(Washer starts to chug and shake.)* But now it's out of order. After four weeks you'd think my husband would get the hint. Course he can't take it into *town* because it costs too much *money*! So what do I do? I just stand here and *hold* it through its cycles. Some automatic! Some husband! *(dance resumes)*

68

'So what do I do? I just stand here and *hold* it through its cycles.'
Front: Miles, Anne   Back: Paul, Fina, David

MARION
Verse two:

And so they got married and a farm they bought.
They was ever so harried and never gave a thought,
As to which one of them would do the heavy farm work.
And who would be happy in the kitchen dirt.
Old fat Hank well now he sat back,
He gave her ten kids and the odd quick whack,
She kept the house and he thought it no harm,
If she minded the kids and she ran the farm.

> *Man in washroom at a dance, finishes his leak and then turns toward the audience to touch up his hair and curl his forelock in the mirror.*

MAN

Yeah, Did you see her? She's the one Bert was telling us about last week. Oh, I don't know ... Janet or something. Yeah, I tell you. She gets you out on the dance floor and pushes those tubes right through to your shoulder blades. I'm getting right back out there and see if I can take her home. She's a sure thing! *(dance resumes)*

MARION
Verse three:

Well, the day came round, it was Fred's birthday,
But she had no money for a cake to pay,
Now about this dilemma Maisy got to thinkin'
While Fred sat in the kitchen, beer drinkin'.
Friday night, she got him to take her
To the auction in Clinton to buy a cake-maker,
They sat thru the night till miscellaneous,
And she sold Hank for ten bucks instantaneous.

WOMAN

(with amorous undertone) My husband is out *working* in the fields for ten, twelve maybe sixteen hours a day. And of course it keeps him in good condition. But he's *tired* when he gets home. Now it's not as if I don't have a lot to *do* around the house, with the kids and the house and all, but well I *miss* him.

MARION
(stands up in washing machine for conclusion)
Well, she had her cake and she had her man,
And she had ten kids and a frying pan.
And now old Maisy she is 84.
But she ain't lookin' for a man no more.

Clap and hoot, exit all: intermission.

Act II, Scene I. Jean Lobb.

Actress enters, sits on milk can, stage centre, quiets the audience and begins.

JEAN LOBB

I'm Mrs Jean Lobb and I live with my husband, Mervyn, and my son, Gordon, on the 16th line. I live quite close to the old school house that they don't use any more.

I was sitting at the back of the church at Fay Merrill's wedding. That was in July. Now there was something that I thought was very lovely about it. I was standing up as the girls came up the aisle, and Jeanette (that's my daughter) was standing up at the front. Now she was going to sing. Now here, the girls were coming up the aisle. There was Karen Oakes and then Lois Merrill in her bridesmaid's outfit, and I didn't know the next girl, and then there was Fay. Now this is a group of girls that had played together as kids; you know what I mean? And great pals, and it was one of their big days, it was something. Now they couldn't all be there. Marilyn Tebbutt had had her uh, twins that week – so *she* couldn't be there. Now Patty Tebbutt's wedding was last year and I don't just know if she was there or not, but this is a group of girls that have been married in the last two years. Jeanette started the ball rolling in February. And then there was Patty – no, Lois, and *then* Patty and then Marilyn. Four girls in the community. And this year there was Fay, and then there's Karen Oakes. *Six* girls, in *two* years, in *one* little community. Well!

Now, at *their* wedding – now it's funny how you think of things, but every detail had to be just *so*. Yes. Now Fay wanted red at her wedding. Well, so did Marilyn. Marilyn wanted her wedding late in the year, last year, Marilyn Tebbuttt, so she could have red in her wedding. Now at Fay's wedding the girls' bridesmaids outfits were the white with the red, and then Lulu (that's Fay's mother) put red geraniums in the girls' bouquets, to bring out the red. Yeah. And it was very precise. Everything was just so. And that's the way they planned Lois's wedding too, and that's the way they wanted it.

Well, we wanted ours different. We're different. Now Jeanette was married at the end of February. Well, that's as fast as we could get ready. We made our wedding clothes, she made her wedding dress; and we were married in the little Baptist church in town – *she* was. Oh, now this wedding album is very nice. Jeanette gave us this for Christmas, because we didn't have the pictures of her wedding, and she put *our* wedding picture at the front of this book. Now for *my* wedding we went out into the garden and we picked our flowers. There was dutzia and roses and we were given the delphiniums, and there was a big white satin bow around them, and when the day was done, well so were they. But whose last much longer? It was the *colours* we wanted. Now she put a picture of each of the children in my family, that have been married so far. That's Bruce's wedding there. There's Hugh. And Murray ... And, oh here's Jeanette! Now she *made* this wedding dress. It was a cream lace over a shrimp pink background. She looked lovely. Now our wedding was a little more informal than a lot of weddings. Well, there wasn't time! Two months! *(laughs)*

Oh boy, I wish I could have had it this year because I had an operation last year in May, and they remodelled and removed so much that I am greatly improved! Ha! ha! ha! Oh, it's *awful* to begin your life at sixty two.

Oh, now let's see, here's a cute thing they did. Right after the service they went over to this little table and there were these two candles that were lit and this taller one in the middle wasn't. They each picked up a candle and they lit the one in the middle and then they blew the other two out. Well, it was something they saw at another service somewhere. The preacher wasn't too keen, no. But then they went right over to another table and they signed the register and all the papers right there. And you know, it saved a lot of *time*. And there's nothing *wrong* in doing something *different*. No.

I don't have any pictures from the wedding dinner, but that was really something. Now at most wedding dinners you have your toasts and they have dinner and a few speeches and everybody goes home. Well, not her! She decided she wanted to have all her brothers to participate because you see only Gordon was an usher. Now there's Don and Bruce and Murray and Hugh. Those are her brothers. Now Don is the oldest, and he represented her baby days and they pinned a diaper on him and they sang one of those songs, you know the song about the kid, the beautiful kid, what's that song – 'I must have been a beautiful baby 'cause baby, look at me now' ... ha! ha! ha! They sang that. And then there was Bruce. Now Bruce is *six feet tall*, and he represented her when she was a little girl and she had braids. Well, they found a hat with a brim on it and they pinned the braids onto the hat, and he wore that. And then they had another silly song. And oh, they found a red bikini bathing suit for Murray to represent her when she was a teenager. And at the *last* minute he couldn't get up the *courage* to put it on. Ha! ha! ha! Well they found him a *wig* or something, and then they had another little doodiddle. And then

there was Hugh, with a suitcase – the days when she'd be travelling.
And then they *all* got up with Gordon and they *all* sang. Well, we
laughed till we died at the *stupidity* of it. It was simple you know, but it
was *so* funny.

LOBB SONG
Verse one:
When Mervyn sang tenor in the old church choir,
There came an eager lady who would him inspire,
To sing in parts the best there can be,
Soon he learned to sing to her, marry me, mary me.

Then it started growing, that old Lobb tree,
Don and Bruce, Murray and Hugh, Gord and Jeannie.
They all grew straight and tall and strong,
And all settled down around Clinton town, Clinton town.

CHORUS
Mobs of Lobbs, Lobb-in-laws, ready-on-the job Lobbs
All along the Maitland and the 16th line.
If you go out driving there, any time,
Looking out your window you too will see
That ever-spreading, farming, Lobb dynasty, dynasty.

JEAN
Oh well, I guess some people just do things differently than others.
(exit)

Act II, Scene II. Daisie.

DAISIE

Oh, it's terrible. I remember when my daughter, Mary, was just a little thing, just about six years old, and her cousin was a year younger. Well, they got playing down at the bottom of the orchard and the cousin fell in the little bucket thing and Mary pulled her out. Oh, yes, she pulled her out. I remember, she came in like this, just dripping! But Mary pulled her out. Oh, you had to be prepared for emergencies in those days. Even now, I know, there's a man, he doesn't live ... he bought the house across the road ... and he works till twelve o'clock at night I hear that tractor. And as long as I hear it – well ... that's fine. But when it's stopped! Oh, I get so nervous, to think that maybe it has rolled over on him ... because there's been a good many people around here that's been killed on them. Especially going around these hills, they'll just flip over ... they're not safe, they're not!

Now, I know, there was a man ... he went out after his lunch, and his wife wondered why he didn't come in, and there he was, dead under it! It had rolled over, and he was pinned under it. And then there was a hurricane around here a couple of years ago and neighbours of ours, their house and their garden and everything was demolished. And so ... the man went back in the fields to get something. Well, he got stuck! So he called his wife to come out to see if she could drive the tractor so he could work it. Well, they hit something, and she fell off, and she fell face down in the mud, and there was just enough air for her to breath, or she would have suffocated! They had to go to another farm to get a tractor to pull it off her. Oh, it was terrible, her arm was broke and her chest was crushed – that can happen!

Farming isn't a ..., it isn't ..., and then there was a man killed by a tree. Ya. Cox was out cuttin' the trees and a branch fell and it just happened to be the mid-term holiday, and the boys was with him, and a branch fell and it took out his eye and all the skin on the side of his face. And so the boys (and they were just boys from school) they ran and got a tractor, and took him to Victoria. And he lived for six weeks like that, and never became conscious. And died. Well, it was a great big dead elm you see, and if it had hit him on top of the head it wouldn't have been so bad, but it struck him right on the side of the face. They said he never would have been mentally right, his brain was so badly damaged. Oh, that can happen! *(exit)*

Act II, Scene III. Accident.

MAN

(enters followed by three neutral actors) Sure, farming's dangerous. With the machinery and heavy implements. You take a baler, for example, with its rows of rotating steel rakes and heavy cutting knives and a huge plunger arm which shoves the bales up to be loaded on the wagon. I remember in 1959 my Uncle Carman was haying and usually his wife drove the tractor, but on this particular day she had to go into Clinton for some reason or another and so he phoned up to ask if I could drive for him. So I went down and we were baling in the field behind his barn. We had baled about two wagon loads I guess, and had piled the bales in the mow ... *(Two actors become baler with appropriate sounds. The third becomes Uncle Carman loading bales.)* and we were working on the third wagon and we had it about half built. We were working on the rise on the west side and the motor was lugging so that I couldn't hear anything except the tractor *(pinging sound from baler)* and suddenly my Uncle shouted at me to stop. I pulled the tractor out of gear and brought back the throttle, and my uncle jumped off the wagon and came around by the rakes of the baler. *(Actors enact story as it unfolds.)* There was a pinging sound in the rakes. A stone or something had got caught in the housing. Very carefully, he worked the stone free from the housing with a screwdriver, and he was just coming away from the baler when he noticed some straw caught in the sprocket of the plunger arm. He started to reach for it, just when the tractor started to stall. He shouted at me to speed up the tractor. I brought *up* the throttle! And the plunger arm came down heavily on the right side of his face *(Carman screams, falls back)* caught his eye, nose, cheek ...

I didn't say anything. Just ran back to the farm house. He was conscious all the way to London. *(Carman carefully carried off stage right by narrator and actors who previously composed the baler)*

WOMAN

(on the verge of tears enters stage left) People have been just wonderful since the accident. The day the accident happened people I didn't even know brought food and everything. The people down the road are looking after my two small children. The one and the three-year-olds, and, well, that's a load off my mind, right now ...

It was a head injury. The machine hit him on the head and he hasn't regained consciousness yet. They've done X-rays and all, but they can't tell from that how long it will be. The farm is such a problem, it's difficult for me to get all the work done. And I just don't know ...

My twelve-year-old has just been wonderful. He milks the cows, and helps me with the housework, and this morning ... he washed the floor.

The day *after* the accident, you could see about *twelve* tractors out in that field, and they had the whole thing done in a *day*. *(exit)*

'These brutes are wheel to wheel. So it's up to *you*, the farm implement buying public, to decide who's going home with that coveted Acre-Eater Award!'
Paul, David, Miles

Act II, Scene IV. Tractor Tug.

ANNOUNCER
(enters carrying reversed hammer for microphone) Ladies and Gentlemen, welcome to the 1973 International Plowing Match! We have added a special attraction for you today – we know you will enjoy it! This is ... the *gargantuan war* of the *tractors*! *(Tractors begin to move out)* You can see them now. Moving out. Perhaps, as they are warming up, we may have an opportunity to speak with these two wonderful contestants – we'll see what we can do. Excuse me. *(doing warm-up exercises, lifting bales, working his 'hydraulics', etc.)*

FARMALL
Ahhhh! *Never, never*, sneak up behind any International Harvester Farm-All 656, boy!

ANNOUNCER
Sorry, I wasn't thinking ... ah, tell me, and also the viewing public, how you *feel* about this upcoming struggle?

FARMALL
I'm ready to take the King – today is *the* day. We Farm-Alls work twelve months of the year – too busy to do much loafing. Get a load of this hydraulic lift, will ya.

ANNOUNCER
So you are actually confident that you will beat the champ.

FARMALL
That's right. I *know* I will. He's been on top too long – time he was dethroned. *(retreats to warm up silently)*

ANNOUNCER
Well, it's good to see such confidence in a young tractor – good luck out there! That was the International Harvester 656 and now we may have the opportunity to speak to the long-time champ, the Case ...

AGRIKING
Agriking seven seventy rrrrrrrr!

ANNOUNCER
Well, tell me, Mr King, I've just spoken to your opponent, and he seems quite confident of victory – how do you feel about that?

AGRIKING

That's all part of that psychological warfare they picked up from the Russians during the Team Canada series, but *nothing replaces power, performance, action*! My mechanic says I've never been in better shape!

ANNOUNCER

Tell me, as long-time champ, do you have any advice for young tractors on their way to the top?

AGRIKING

(shifts to natural voice) Well, Howard, the trouble with young tractors today is they *just* don't *know* what they *want*! We *give* them *everything*. We give them tinted glass, three-speed air conditioning, accoustical padding, *ashtrays*. We even sent one little garden tractor on a tour of China! But they still don't want to be *tractors*! RRRR!

ANNOUNCER

Great words from a great champ – good luck out there! Well, you've seen them, you heard them, and now it's time. It's the moment thousands have waited for – a clash of *giants*! They're moving up to the rope now. At this end of the rope, weighing in at 2,452 pounds in the red and cream enamel trunks, the Farmall! And at this end of the rope, weighing in at 2,654 pounds in the power red and desert sunset enamel trunks, the Case Agriking! We should get the signal from the reeve to begin. Do we have a delay? No, we will begin … *(BONG! strikes pipe or whatever with his hammer)*

AGRIKING

Agriking! Purrs like a kitten. Steers like a dream. Works like a *horse*!

Double rear wheel traction pulls you up those steep grades through those tough spots!

Twelve forwards gears, synchro-mesh clut'ch, fluid drive transmission, Sixty-three

FARMALL
The Farmall 656 is light, lean, and *tough*!

Ten forward gears, two reverse! The slickest shiftin' tractor you've ever seen.

Optional power torque amplifier allows you to decrease speed and increases power by forty-five percent giving you sixty-plus horsepower. Torsion bar draft

horsepower with torque multiplying planetaries Case cube reserve power! RRRRRRR! etc.

controlled hitch to raise and lower both heavy and light implements. Shift gears without stopping – a tremendous asset in this heavy clay soil! RRRRRRR! etc.

ANNOUNCER

(Bong! Bong!) Well, I imagine you are as breathless as I am. Knowing that tractor history was made out here today. But, as you can see, it's a *stand-off*! These brutes are wheel to wheel. So it's up to *you*, the farm implement buying public, to decide who's going home with that coveted Acre-Eater Award! Only your applause can send home a champion ... How about the long-time champ, the *Agriking*!

Applause.

How about this honest, good-hearted challenger from south-western Ontario, the *Farmall*!

Applause.

Well, folks, the _____ takes it home!

A saw-off in applause can be settled by appealing to an individual member of the audience or by simply leaving it that way. Obviously this scene allows considerable leeway for improvisation.

LOBB SONG

Verse two:

Bruce saw Diane waiting on tables and
When she brought him coffee, spilled it over his knee.
Oh, how he burned for her until one day
He bought a wedding ring for her and stole her away, stole her away.
Then it started growing that old Lobb tree
Michael, Christopher, Jacka a bundle of three
They're learning their Bible and they know God's way
Will lead them to another family someday.

CHORUS:

Mobs of Lobbs, Lobb-in-laws, etc.

Ted Johns as Farmall

Act II, Scene v. Jesus Bus.

*As the actors recreate the action, the somewhat humorous
predicament of the bus works in counterpoint to Diane's natural and
direct narration. Action slows or ceases entirely during the speeches of
the witness building in the audience's mind a series of latent images
resembling the stations of the cross. These three planes of expression
(Diane, Witness, Bus) come together around Diane during the
hymn, allowing her prayer considerable force of sincerity.*

DIANE

You've probably seen our bus around Clinton. It's a great big London
double-decker bus and we've painted 'JESUS EQUALS PEACE' on the
top deck.

BUS

Jesus equals Peace.

WITNESS

We'd like to welcome all of you here tonight. We're so happy that our
new Drive-in church is drawing more and more people to an
awareness of God.

DIANE

Well, we had the bus shipped from London to Halifax, and then
Bruce and I and the Gellings and another couple, Bob and Carol
Stevenson, who owned the bus went to Halifax to pick it up. And we
really felt that God was with us throughout the entire journey.

WITNESS

There are just four steps to salvation. The first step is to recognize that
you are a sinner.

DIANE

When we got to Halifax, we picked up the bus, but then we
discovered that we needed a special permit to buy the diesel fuel for it.
But at the very first gas station we went into, the attendant thought we
were one of the tourist buses from around Halifax, so he filled up our
tank. And then he discovered that we weren't them, but he just wrote
something on the top of the bill, and from then on we used that bill
whenever we needed to buy diesel fuel.

'You've probably seen our bus around Clinton. It's a great big London double-decker bus and we've painted JESUS EQUALS PEACE on the top deck.' *Janet, Miles, David, Fina, Anne*

WITNESS

The second step is to recognize that you cannot save yourself. Until you can accept that, there is no hope of your being saved.

DIANE

Well, we got outside of Halifax and the bus broke down. *(choking sounds from actor portraying bus)* The radiator had dried out – and there we were. We were in the middle of nowhere; there were no houses around, no cars on the road, we were miles from the nearest town, and we had no water on the bus with us. We didn't know what we were going to do. And then, we discovered that on the other side of the bus, just by the road, there was a stream! So we filled up our radiator and continued on our way.

WITNESS

The third step is to believe that Jesus Christ died on the cross bearing our sins.

DIANE

Well, we only had one more break-down on the way to Ottawa – and that was when the fanbelt broke. But it turned out to be a very good thing that the fanbelt *had* broken, because if it hadn't, the entire motor would have gone! And we really felt that God was protecting us from disaster. And we got all the way to Ottawa, we got into Ottawa, and then the bus broke down again!

WITNESS

I would like to witness for you and tell you the story of my own salvation. All my life I was a sinner, but I thought I was a good person and I was trying to do the right thing. Then I got very ill, and I was lying sick in bed when it came to me that my whole life was sick with sin. And as soon as I realized that, something inside of me just let go, and I was filled with more peace and joy than I had ever known in my whole life. And that took me to the fourth step. To accept Jesus Christ as your own personal saviour.

DIANE

Well, we couldn't get the bus fixed in Ottawa for three or four days, so we made plane reservations to fly home. Well, our children were staying with relatives, mine with my mother-in-law. And then Bruce and Hank were just fiddling around with the bus, and they discovered that all it needed was new ball bearings. And someone said they knew of a store, we phoned them up and they said they'd stay open for us. Bruce and Hank rushed down! – well, we didn't think we were going to get the ball bearings – it's an English bus. But they went down anyway, and Bruce gave the number of the ball bearings to the man, and he just turned around and picked a whole box of exactly the right ball bearings right off the shelf behind him! And Bruce and Hank rushed back to the bus and we got it fixed, and of course, we missed our plane, but that was all right because the bus was fixed and we set off for Clinton the next morning. And we got within 20 miles of Clinton, we got to Mitchell – and then the bus broke down again! And this time, we had to leave the bus in Mitchell and go home to Clinton on our own, and we were *so* disappointed.

> *Witness softly begins hymn and the other actors assemble around her forming a choir which gradually builds in volume during the following lines:*

But we thought about it (*moves downstage*) afterwards, and we realized that God was trying to tell us that the the glory belonged to Him. That the glory of bringing the bus into Clinton belonged to God. And since then we take the bus out on weekends to the beaches at Bayfield and Goderich, and we witness, and we hand out tracts, and last Sunday we saved three people!

HYMN
Let Jesus come into your heart
Jesus he knows the way
Sinners repent and rejoice
Jesus is here today.

Jesus come in
Into our hearts today
Jesus he is the light
Jesus is here to stay.

DIANE
And now, if I may, I would like to say a short prayer with you all.

Lord Jesus, we come to thee as sinners.
Help us to here and now repent of all our many sins.
Show us that we cannot save ourselves, but that
Thou didst die on the cross bearing our sins for us.
Let us open our hearts to thee,
And accept thee as our own personal saviour,

And thank thee for saving us.
Amen.

WITNESS

I'd like to say how glad I am to see all of you here tonight. I hope that those of you who have come for the first time have found something new to take home with you. And for those who come every week, I hope this evening has brought you, once again, close to Jesus.

Actors exit quietly during Lobb Song.

LOBB SONG
Verse three:
Don and Alison met on a farm in Ridgetown
She was cleaning kennels, grooming horses to show
He was assistant manager but found a little time for her
Before agriculture school they thought they'd make a go,
thought they'd make a go,
Then it started growing that old Lobb tree
Steven, David, Robin, all boys they be
They all hate girls and much prefer their hockey
But in time I'm sure they'll climb up the Lobb tree,
up the Lobb tree.

CHORUS
Mobs of Lobbs, Lobb-in-laws, etc.

Act II, Scene VI. Alison Lobb.

MAN *(mimes)*
A farm kitchen.
Big. Open. Bright.
A window.
A refrigerator,
Counter, sink, and
A stove.

WOMAN *(mimes)*
Table.
Gleaming. Smooth. White.
A picture: autumn leaves, a bridge, a horse
And in the foreground,
Two, tiny, white
Ducks.

ALISON
(enters briskly, mimes kitchen work during her speech) Hi, I'm Alison Lobb. This house you're looking at we've just moved into. We were burned out of our other place about three years ago. Actually there's just one bedroom upstairs that needs further work. You know, it's a strange thing about that room. There are about forty to sixty holes in the walls. And we can't for the life of us figger out why anybody would want to have so many holes in the walls. However. There are three bedrooms up there and our three boys are in the largest. When we first got married, we only wanted one. But I'd like more. I would. I'd like a girl. And I know how to get one too. There was an article in Nova magazine a few weeks ago and they explained how you could get a girl. You know – with timing and frequency and that sort of thing. And you know, it's really true! Because looking back, I can see how all ours turned out to be boys. However.

I don't think that nowadays a woman with a large family has to stay inside all the time. I really don't. You have your vacuum cleaner and your washer and your car. Well, most women don't have automatic washers, but I don't like washing dishes, so I just stack them up and leave them, and at the end of the day I do them. And that's fine. Nobody seems to mind. Don's mother will look after the kids. You know, I'm really fortunate to have her because I could never afford to pay a babysitter. A few years ago I decided that I wanted to teach.

And so, I thought, 'Well I'll teach Sunday School and see if I like it.' Well I guess I do, because I'm still doing it. I'm not religious. You might even say that I border on the agnostic. But I'm superintendent of the Sunday School and treasurer of the Church and president of the Ladies Guild.

You know what bothers me? People will send their kids to Sunday School and have no idea what they're being taught. None. They just think, 'Well, if I send my kid to Sunday School, then I'm doing the right thing.' Now, I teach those kids comparative religions, and if there were synagogues in town to take them to, I would. But nobody cares. The Ladies Guild is run pretty much like a general meeting. Minutes, a treasurer's report, and a prayer – one at the beginning and one at the end. We meet once a month and we'll have a talk, or a penny sale. Or if somebody's been some place and they want to show their slides, well, we'll have that. But most of the women around here aren't particularly interested in good works. They just want to get together and talk. Gossip. Well, if that's what they want to do. Fine. I let them. I do believe, though, that you've got to take the initiative. And I do this. And maybe I'm criticized for it but if I am, I haven't *heard* about it. But I think if you're going to take the initiative, you're bound to get criticism. So it doesn't bother me.

But there was an example of this being necessary. The principal of a public school in town, John Siertsema was his name, was being transferred and everyone wanted to do something for him. So they had this picnic and they fiddled and tiddled and diddled about and nothing got done! So finally, I got together with Marlene Forbes and Millie Lobb and Sally Bird. And Sally got the idea to do a skit, so we said, 'Fine, you do it,' and she did. She did the costumes and the scenery and everything. And it was really good. They called it 'To Sierts with Love'. The students performed it. Then Marlene Forbes sent out the invitations, and Millie Lobb, we're really fortunate to have her, because she wrote a poem and it was published in the paper. And I bought the presents, and of course, the other women helped with the tea and coffee and that sort of thing, so it was really successful. *(checks meat in stove)* Back in 1967 I was invited to sit on the township council and this was a wonderful experience because I learned so much about how things were run. I represented our community in the township for the centennial celebrations. And I think what we did was really good. The school in Holmesville was an antique display. And everybody who had any antiques submitted them to the school. There was a Dutch room, for instance. There are a lot of Dutch people around here and they submitted handicrafts, maps and symbols of their culture and everyone who had old clothes handed them in, and the women modelled them and even some of the little girls, and that was really cute. Then we had a parade. I think that's the *best* parade I've ever seen! There were forty floats and three prizes for the best. Don's float was just a scream. It was a bathhouse float. Don was sitting in this bath tub and the other fellas, Jack Tebbutt, Alvin, Murray and Bill, were sloshing water over him, and over the spectators because they were drinking out of these jugs and it wasn't exactly water they were drinking. By the time the parade got rolling they were half cut. Then there was an out-house on it, and someone would go inside and slosh water around so it looked like someone had missed the seat! Needless to say we didn't win. Then there was a ball game and Don's team wore braids and grass skirts. On Sunday there was a service and I sang in the choir.

It was really good.

Of course, there's a lot to do around the farm. I do all Don's books. Originally he wanted me to do this because I'm from Toronto and he thought it would help me to understand the cash-flow. And it has. And I know that if anything happened to Don, I could cope. I could

(Enter Stephen carrying guitar)
Stephen, take off your rubbers. I thought I told you.

STEPHEN
When's supper?

ALISON
Six o'clock. *(Stephen grimaces.)* Well, make yourself a sandwich. Kids! *(Or work out alternative ending depending on guitarist)*

LOBB SONG
Verse four:
Mervyn's brother Jim farmed property
That had a school upon it so he looked to see
Verna, the teacher there and, whoops!, there was gone
Another teacher from the board of education.
Then it started growing that old Lobb tree
Leonard, Ernie, Eleanor and Tommy
Now Leonard has a farm along Highway 8
And the others are working hard and following fate.

CHORUS
Mobs of Lobbs, Lobb-in-laws, etc.

Act II, Scene VII. Township Council.

The bales are set into place during the Lobb song. Each councilman has a characteristic voice and manner. Before speaking a line attributed to one of the men the actor must quickly move into his place and assume his character. As the convention becomes familiar, the audience tends to watch the places rather then the actors moving about so that it becomes unnecessary for the actor to speak each time he or she moves. No character is consistently played by one actor. In the course of the scene each of the actors plays each of the five men once or several times. Robin's reading, for example, may be continued by one actor moving out and the other moving into his place. The number of combinations is so large that it is best to allow the two actors to work out a rhythm and timing familiar enough to allow some inventiveness at each performance. The bales are set in a square like this:

FIRST ACTOR
(stands and addresses the audience naturally while second sits behind on a bale) We went to two township council meetings. What we expected was a large public meeting something like this *(indicates the stage and audience)* but what we went into was a large room behind a garage with a group of farmers sitting around a table. Now these men do all the business for Hullett township.

They were pretty surprised to see us and asked if we had any questions. We said, 'No. But could we sit and watch?" This is an impression of the two meetings we saw. *(sits down and assumes character)*

LITTLE GUY
What do you *mean* we don't know who owns the schoolhouse?

EVERT
Well, Robin here says he can't find the deed!

ROBIN
That's right, but if you would like me to go back and look again, I'll see if I can't find some ownership papers or deeds or something.

JAKE
Well, we can't sell it to those T.V. station people if we don't have a title. Some sharpy lawyer from Toronto will come up here and ... I move we put this off till next week.

EVERT
It's been moved we put this off till next week ... Do we have a seconder?

JAKE
I'll second it.

EVERT
It's been moved and seconded, we put this off till next week, all in favour? *(Wayne yawns)* Yeah, Wayne, you're in favour ...

ROBIN
I'd like to take care of this *municipal* drain question ...

EVERT
Robin, I'd like to take care of that *municipal* drain question if I may. Oh, oh you're *on* to it.

ROBIN
I'd like to get on ... etc. *(reads in a monotone from profile printed at the end of this scene. Others interrupt at various intervals with the following remarks)*

JAKE
Now this is an *improvement*, not a *replacement*, we've spent money for the same things before and ...

LITTLE GUY
I thought it was a new drain!

JAKE
Is that Roberts' fella, the engineer coming?

EVERT
No, he's on holiday in California!

LITTLE GUY
Gee, I wish *I* could go to California.

JAKE
Let's see, now, following along on these profiles ... I see ... 35 plus 80 ... uh ... I'm lost ... uh, Robin ... where are we, do I go downstream now?

ROBIN

That's right, downstream …

JAKE

Oh, is this my willow tree?

ROBIN

No, that's William's elm tree.

JAKE

Oh. I see … Wayne, are you following along on these profiles?

WAYNE

(*yawning*) No, I never follow along, they don't … (*mumble*)

LITTLE GUY

Why didn't that engineer send his son, he's an engineer too. We're gonna need someone to answer questions, you know …

ROBIN

'My estimate of the cost is as follows …'

JAKE

Now just a minute, now … Evert, you're on top of that cost thing, now what's that gonna cost us all told?
Two actors stare at Evert's empty seat and nod.
Uh, huh … (*pause*)

ROBIN

Uh, huh. That's about right.

EVERT

(*together with Jake, below*) That means it's going to cost twice as much as it did last time, and they're not even using any bulldozers!

JAKE

(*together with Evert, above*) Well, I don't think we should *spend* that kind of money. We're not going to get anything out of it anyway.

WAYNE

(*jumps to alertness at last*) My God!

JAKE

(together with Little Guy, below) The engineer shoulda had a representative here to answer questions. He's getting paid a lot of money for this.

LITTLE GUY

Does anybody want a Pepsi? *(Robin reads on)*

JAKE

(to Wayne) Yeah Wayne you need a Crispy Crunch to keep up your strength. *(Robin reads on)*

JAKE

(interrupting Robin again, this time with a real problem) Now, going back a bit, Robin. You said Station 10, plus zero, zero, and then back a bit, Station 85 plus 5. Now what's the difference?

ROBIN

Eleven feet. *(reads on)*

LITTLE GUY

Now Keith Fennel's not going to get away with that this year! He says he doesn't need a drain in there at the back of his property because the water drains off naturally.

WAYNE

(cuts in) There's *no way* that water's going to drain uphill, ha! ha!

LITTLE GUY

We'll have to hear from Keith about that.

JAKE

Well, if we don't hear from *him* we'll hear from his *wife*!

There is laughter from everyone. Two actors jump quickly from seat to seat showing different laughters. Robin reads on.

WAYNE

Anybody knows what *time* it is?

LITTLE GUY

What's on the late movie anyway?

Lobb Song cuts in: freeze.

LOBB SONG
Verse five:
Mervyn's cousin Alma can be seen.
Caring for her garden and her fine cuisine.
When her son moved to Goderich to paint a house,
He drove a business lady home and found him a spouse.
Then it started growing that old Lobb tree
Now they're raising pigs and raspberries
With Susan and Jerry, Brian and Valerie.

CHORUS:
Mobs of Lobbs, Lobb-in-laws, etc.

During the Lobb song, the actors remove the bales.

TOWNSHIP COUNCIL PROFILE
(This is what Robin reads from)
I'd like to get on to this improvement to the municipal drain, if I
may. I only have one copy of the letter, so I'll have to read that to
you but you can follow along on the profiles which I'll hand out.
Now, this drain was built eleven years ago and it's silted up and it's
not doing the job it's supposed to. 'Should provide a better
self-draining action from station ten plus zero, zero to the outlet into
the creek at Station 85 plus 55. The drain has been extended
downstream for an addition of 555 feet beyond the original
construction. This work was made necessary by the silt which has
partially filled the existing channel between the outlet of the original
work and the present outlet. The farm culvert at Station 35 plus 80
and the culvert at Station 65 plus 45 on the sideroad between 35 and
26 must be lowered to conform with the grade line established by
the profile. The pipes shall be back-filled as closely to the present
site of repair as possible. It is intended that the pipes shall have the
invert set at three inches below grade. I determine the amounts to be
paid in allowances to the owners entitled thereto under the drainage
act as follows:

Township of Hullet, Concession 2, Lot 26, J. Rapson, Damages to
lands and crops $20.00
Goderich Township, Concession 17, Lot 24 and 25, Red Baddon
$65.00.

North west sixty acres on Lot 26, William Jenkins $85.00 Lot 27 of
Concession 17, William Jenkins, $65.00.
North half of Lot 28 on Concession 17, William Jenkins, $15.00 .
South half of Lot 28 on Concession 17, Donald Andrews, $30.00.
Total allowances payable, $280.00.

My estimate of the cost of work is as follows:
Work in Hullet Township: 200 cubic yards of
excavation, including removal of brush trees
and cleaning culverts: $115.00
Spreading of excavated materials: $15.00
Estimated cost of the work in Hullett Township: $130.00
Goderich Township. Estimated cost of the work
including removal of brush trees and clearing culverts: $2,300.00
… Owners are responsible for pollutants.
… Payable within thirty days after the one third ($1/3$) subsidy has
been received by the Township.

Act II, Scene VIII. Picture Frame.

Actors stand in a row, framed by large picture frame.

HUSBAND
This farm has been in our family for a long time now. I think it was my grandfather who came over from England and bought a lot of eighty acres along the Maitland in the 1860s. My cousin is making up a book ...

WIFE
There's a picture in there of the log cabin they built in 1862.

HUSBAND
They had to pull the cedars out of the swamp and without machinery they had to ...

FIRST GIRL
(While she speaks she moves out of the frame and into the audience stage left. Others freeze.) I just finished my grade 13 and I decided I don't want to go to university. I've got a job in London working for an insurance company, London Life. I'm sharing an apartment with a couple of friends of mine. I'm really looking forward to it because I've never lived off the farm before. I don't know if I'll come back to the farm again or not.

HUSBAND
This stone house you're looking at our grandfather built. We put in the plumbing and the electricity.

WIFE
Oh you wouldn't know the dampness of it now ... not with the way he's fixed it with the wood panelling and all.

SECOND GIRL
(While she speaks she moves out of the frame and into the audience stage right. Others freeze.) Several years ago, I met a boy and we decided we wanted to get married. Well, my parents didn't like him and we fought, and I left home. We're living in Toronto now and I haven't been back for almost two years.

HUSBAND

We've added a lot of land, we've gone more into livestock than my father did.

WIFE

I have my own source of income from the chickens.

HUSBAND

Of course with the price of machinery what it is now I don't know...

WIFE

And I mow the lawn.

HUSBAND

Still, it would be nice to be able to hand the farm on.

BOY

(Moves out of the frame and addresses the audience. Others freeze.) I managed, gee I don't know how, to get a scholarship to study English at a university. And I'm going to get my degree and I'm going to be a teacher. I think I'll go up North to teach. I hope my father understands. *(moves out of focus)*

HUSBAND

The kids today don't want to work hard and they've got the T.V. and everything telling them how they can live in the city and make a lot of money.

WIFE

Oh, they'll work. But even if they did want to buy the farm, we'd be dead by the time they got enough money. Oh yes. Of course you know it's not easy, you just can't hand your farm down to your children. There's taxes to pay, and the government ...

HUSBAND

Succession taxes, and the forms that they make you fill out make it very difficult ...

WIFE

I think farming is the best of both worlds though. You can go into town when you want and ... *(cut off by auctioneer, freeze)*

Now let's see what we have here. Oh yes, we have a nice picture,
with a nice hand-crafted picture frame. And well, if you don't *like*
the picture you can cut it out, put in your own, and it would look
good against *anybody's* wall. Well, what'll you give me to start it off?
Anybody give me five …? I got *two, two, two,* – give me a half, got a
half, half, half …
Give me *three, three, three,* got *three*, three, three, give me a *half*? *a
half*? Give me three and a *half*, give me *four, four,* four, give me five!
(etc.)

> *The girls who left the picture frame are now bidding as women in
> the audience. If other members of the audience join in, the price goes
> up until:*

O.K. fella you bought it! Take it away.

LOBB SONG
Verse six:
Murray flew away from high school.
He became a traveller and nobody's fool.
Then when he returned to get his diploma,
He looked around his class and found sweet smiling Robba.
Then Hugh did like his dad and found his Martie
Singing in a choir for our centenary
And then the Mennonites found Jeanette with Ivan
And Gordon's pretty choosy but some day he'll give in,
Some day he'll give in.

CHORUS:
Mobs of Lobbs, Lobb-in-laws, etc.

Act II, Scene IX. Bruce Pallett.

BRUCE

(Actor seats himself squarely on milk can centre stage, confronting audience, high energy.) This is a rotten business! It isn't worth a *damn*, really, y'know? And the only reason we're farming is because – well, it's prob'ly for most of us the only business we know, and we like it, and it's a way of life, eh? And everybody thinks it should be a public utility, and that everybody should supply food for free. It's like this meat boycott and all this garbage.

Now, I don't mind gambling with the weather – well, I mind, but I expect to gamble with the weather, and all that jazz – and the markets – but I don't like fighting the government and the people too, y'know, what the hell – what's it for?

Y'know if we were getting *rich* – y'know the sad part of all this problem they're talking about high food prices, the *sad*, the really *sad* part of it. The people are all uptight about what they call the high cost of food, and the farmers aren't getting enough! Y'know, if the farmers were getting a good shot at it, and the people were bellyachin', well, we'd say to hell with them, let 'em belly-ache! But I'll tell you *this*! If the farmers don't get, I think, *twice* what they're getting in *three* years, then in *five* years, you're gonna be paying *twenty* times as much for food.

Because they're quitting.

Y'see, we're losing agricultural land in Ontario at the rate of forty-three acres an hour. You look at this map of Canada on the back wall. *(illustrates)* This shows all the areas in Canada that'll ever produce food. *Ever*. Not very many is it? Now, look at this narrow strip of land from Windsor to around Montreal. That varies in depth from ten to seventy miles, and that strip of land provides food for almost forty percent of the nation, and that land is disappearing at the rate of forty-three acres an hour. Now, arithmetic was never my strong point, but by rapid calculation that's about a million acres a year.

And that's pretty *fast*, y'know. That's pretty damn *fast*!

And those aren't my figures. That's the census of the Ontario Government and the University of Guelph, they both did it on separate surveys.

You hear people belly-achin' about the price of eggs. You can *buy* an egg for *nine* cents and they scream, but you let their kid yell for a Pepsi and they'll stuff *twenty* cents into a machine.

The average price of a pound of steak in 1971 was $1.46. Now, *if* the price of steaks had increased at the same rate from 1961, for example, as wages, then they should have been worth $2.08 a pound. And if they had increased at the same rate as income tax they should have been $3.80 a pound. If they had increased at the same rate as postage stamps they should have been $1.57 a pound, and if they had increased at the same rate as a newspaper, they should have been $1.75 a pound.

And they're yellin' about meat bein' so expensive. So expensive compared to what? Compared to getting it for damn near nothing, that's what. And they're yellin' about milk. Now, I *know* farmers are getting a fair income on their milk.

And the guy next door to me has just sold his entire dairy herd, and he has an 18 year old son, and he has a *good* farm, and he has just sold every animal he had, and *he* said he could get more money with the thing in *bank interest* than he can foolin' around with *milk*. And they're yellin' about the price of milk!

Y'know, the thing they're tryin' to investigate ... they're lookin' for a bad guy in all this, and I don't know where you're going to find him – unless you go to the average workin' guy. That's only my opinion – 'opinion', prob'ly wrong – but you *take* the average working guy with his Friday night cheque.

He says the only thing he's gonna pay cash for is his booze and his food. So, he writes cheques for his car, his rent or his mortgage, his television, hydro and telephone, and all that jazz, and he has about thirty-six bucks left. So he goes out and he buys a case of beer, little bit of gin, little bit of vodka, and gives the rest to his wife – about twenty-eight bucks. She goes into a supermarket. Well. Seventy-five percent of the women in this country don't know how to shop! They don't know how to cook stew – so she goes in there and buys a T.V. dinner or some silly dumb thing they can't afford, or plastic pails, mops, soap, or panty hose – yeah, *panty hose*. She gets up to the checkout counter, she's two dollars short an' she says the price of *food's* too high!

I'm not an average farmer, so maybe it's not fair to take my example. I sold a farm my grandfather started. I didn't want to sell it but I was in a position where I *had* to sell it because I couldn't live in the city and farm. So I sold it for every lousy buck I could get for it and I don't think there's anybody could find fault with that. Now, I could have taken that money, gone to the Bahamas and said to hell with Canada, eh?

Or, I could have given each of my two kids a hundred thousand bucks when they were twenty-one, and had two complete *fools* when they were 22! A lot of good that would have done the country, eh?

No, I said, 'I'm gonna try and do the right thing and set my two kids up in the farming business.' So, out of all that money I coughed up a quarter of a million bucks, and now instead of seventy acres, I have two hundred acres, and I got it equipped, and I planted an orchard, and it's taken seventeen years to get to the point where it's not quite yet breaking even – now I'll admit we're not at full production yet, my God, we better *not* be!

Y'know, if someone can show me where I'm *wrong*, why I'll listen. I have thirty acres out there I'm not using. I'll rent him that land and *give* him the machinery to work it if he can prove to me that he can produce food for less than I can. Now that's an *offer* and I'll *sign* it!

We have screwy import laws in this country. We had a lot of imported sugar coming in, cheaper than we could produce it, until they shut down all the sugar beet plants in south western Ontario. Now the price of sugar's too high because it's imported. Now, of course, they're fiddling around trying to get the guys back into the sugar beet business. They couldn't have seen *that* ahead of time could they?

Canadian Canners, bought out by Del Monte. Do you know how Del Monte, in the United States, bought out Canadian Canners? They cut the dividends of their shareholders by *one* percent for *one* year ... and bought out Canadian Canners. And now you're buying *imported* food that I could sell you *cheaper*!

Everybody's so damn sure we're making a lot of money, an' all they think about when they see me sellin' apples at four dollars a bushel is, well, 'How many bushels do you grow in a year?' Well, right now, I guess, we produce about twelve or fourteen thousand bushels, an' right away you can see the gears start to turn. Why, the bugger's got seventy thousand *bucks*! That's *right*! In 1971 we sold $73,000 worth of stuff off this farm. But it *took* $73,006.40 to do it! And that's allowing $6,000 for management – that's to keep three families for one year ... each of my kids got three thousand bucks apiece. I didn't get a red cent.

Y'know, I just want my kids to make a *living* at it, I got *grandchildren* I want to make a living at it.

So what else can I *do*? Y'know, how else do you *build* a nation?

'The boys grabbed hold. John slapped her in gear.' *David, Miles*

Act II, Scene x. John Deere.

*With the aid of the other actors the narrator recites
and performs the Ballad of John Deere.*

Ohhh ...
It was years ago, but I remember when,
There weren't no tractors. Just horses, and men!
But all that changed. And I remember the year,
For it was all on account of Big John Deere.

It was down in Clinton off the Maitland way
Where Big John lived and tended his hay.
He grew beans and corn and whatever he could,
And he cared for his family like a good man should.

Many's the day you could travel that road
And hear the groan of his traces as he pulled his load.
He'd work from morn till far in the night
And he farmed that land with all his might.

Till one day he wiped the sweat from his brow
And said there's got to be a better way how
I can farm this land and make it mine,
Without wastin' my effort, my sweat, and my time.

Now John gave 'em all a fright one day
When he drove up to where they was pitchin' hay.
He was sittin' atop an infernal machine
That was spittin' and buckin' and fightin' and mean.

'What is it?' they cried, a backin' away,
'It's a tractor!' said John, 'and it'll change our day.'
Well, I don't know who started laughin' first,
But it just came out in an embarrassin' burst.

They was laughin' and screamin' and holdin' their sides
When John gunned that tractor and spun it out wide.
Then he said nice and gentle with no hurt to see,
'Some day you boys will be ridin' with me.'

Now the day it all happened it was quiet and still.
You'd never think what was brewin' up over that hill.
But the sky split open and the clouds let loose,
And the farmers stood up and cried, 'What the deuce!'

'That's the fastest thunder boomer I've ever seen
And it looks like she's turnin' mighty mean!'
Now the boys had been workin' around John Deere's farm,
So they headed up to his place to wait out the storm.

Now they're sittin' sippin' coffee all cosy and dry,
Swappin' story for story and lie for lie,
When there came a poundin' on the door and a woman's cry!
The door burst open on the Widow Black.
She says, 'My boys are on the river and they can't get back!
Seems they was boatin' on the river when the boomer struck,
Now they're clingin' to a rock and they're just plain stuck!'
So they headed for the river through the rain and the mud
When the feared cry reached 'em, 'Flash Flood!'

So they went back to pullin' their horses through the big barn door
When the air was split by a God-awful roar!
Then lightning struck and lit 'em up fair
And them horses was a-screamin' and pawin' the air.

Now they're feared of that lightnin' and feared of that sound
And them horses weren't movin', just holding' their ground.
Then Jamie Thompson yelled though he was tempest tost,
'We've gotta move these nags or those boys are lost!'

So they went back to tuggin' through the muck and the hay
But them horses weren't movin' – at least not that day.
And the Widow Black despaired, it was plain to see
Cause they needed them horses to get her boys free.

Well, the farmers all figgered the boys' end was near,
But they hadn't counted on big John Deere.
From out of the gloom of that big barn door
Came the sound of an engine and a terrible roar.

And out of that buildin' came a sight for the eye –
Big John's tractor! And him ridin' her high!
He headed for the river with the rain in his face
Kickin' clods and mud at a terrible pace.

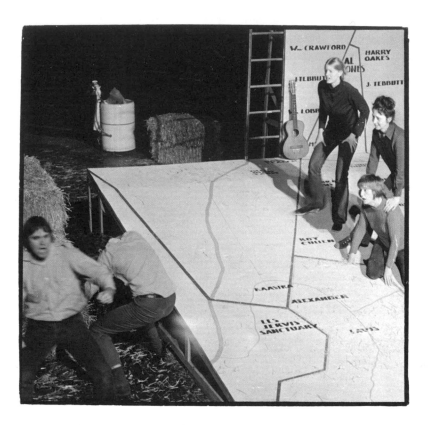

'John kicked her into fightin gear and she began to buck
And at that very moment – high water *struck*!'
Miles, David, Fina, Janet, Anne

He had a rope on his arm, and a fire in his eye.
He was gonna save those boys from the river or die.
But when he reached the banks of that ragin' river,
The boys heads were above water just a tiny little sliver.

So John spun that tractor with almighty ease
And flung that rope out as nice as you please.
The boys grabbed holt. John slapped her in gear.
The whine of that engine was a sound to hear.
And within *five seconds* – those boys were clear!

And the people all shouted, 'He's a hero fair and square!'
Then a little voice spoke up, 'My kitty-cat's out there.'
In old John's mind he had to walk with men.
He had to mount up, and challenge that river again.
And the people cried, 'No John! It ain't no use!'
But he jumped on that tractor and he gave her the juice.

He went into the river, tractor and all,
Him in the saddle and he's ridin' her tall.
We'll never know how but he reached that stone
And snatched up that kitten before she was gone.

Then a voice cried out, 'White water upstream!'
And the rest all happened like a terrible dream.
John whipped off his belt and stropped that kitten down
While the water rushed down like God's own frown.

John kicked her into fightin' gear and she began to buck.
And at that very moment – high water *struck*!
Well, a few moments later, oh I don't know how,
That tractor came clear, easy as pullin' a plow,

With a kitty on board, all scared and wet,
But no sign of John – we ain't seen one yet.
Some say he pulled himself ashore below
And he's savin' kittens still – but I don't know.

But one thing come of that fateful day
And I'm proud that I can stand here and say,
'Whenever men gather, be it far or near,
And there's a tractor of that make – men named her, *John Deere*.

THE END OF THE PLAY

NOTES

NOTES

Coach House Printing Company
401 Huron Street on bpNichol Lane
Toronto, Ontario M5S 2G5
(416) 979-2217
http://www.chbooks.com

NOTES